Dark Persuasion

The Ultimate Guide to Understand NLP Persuasion Psychology, Practice Dark Psychology and the Art of Manipulation to Defend Oneself

© Copyright 2019 - All rights reserved.

The content contained within this book may not be reproduced, duplicated or transmitted without direct written permission from the author or the publisher.

Under no circumstances will any blame or legal responsibility be held against the publisher, or author, for any damages, reparation, or monetary loss due to the information contained within this book. Either directly or indirectly.

Legal Notice:

This book is copyright protected. This book is only for personal use. You cannot amend, distribute, sell, use, quote or paraphrase any part, or the content within this book, without the consent of the author or publisher.

Disclaimer Notice:

Please note the information contained within this document is for educational and entertainment purposes only. All effort has been executed to present accurate, up to date, and reliable, complete information. No warranties of any kind are declared or implied. Readers acknowledge that the author is not engaging in the rendering of legal, financial, medical or professional advice. The content within this book has been derived from various sources.

Please consult a licensed professional before attempting any techniques outlined in this book.

By reading this document, the reader agrees that under no circumstances is the author responsible for any losses, direct or indirect, which are incurred as a result of the use of information contained within this document, including, but not limited to, — errors, omissions, or inaccuracies.

Table of Contents

Introduction

Congratulations on downloading *Dark Persuasion* and thank you for doing so.

The following chapters will discuss many subjects related to Dark Persuasion, Dark Psychology, manipulation, and other topics. In our modern world, we are subjected to Dark Psychological principles and Dark Persuasion in many ways. Being able to understand these principles will make you much more difficult to take advantage of. This book will present information relevant to your own protection as well as how to use these principles in your favor when necessary.

With all those books about the subject flooding the market, we appreciate picking this book! Information found in this has been checked and made sure that it is useable and accurate. Please enjoy!

Chapter 1: NLP (Neuro-Linguistic Programming)

Neuro-Linguistic Programming, or NLP, can be defined as "the study of subjective experience". Let's break that down into parts, shall we? First of all, the "study" means that we are looking at something in order to understand it. Geology is the study of the earth, and so on. In order to study something like subjective experience, there must be a breadth of study methods employed. After all, studying subjective experience is a lot different than studying certain plants, animals, or natural features. "Subjective experience" covers a wide swathe of human expression, thinking, feeling, and all sorts of other aspects of our existence. Subjective experience is something that each of us has, and it is almost impossible to completely understand and convey the subjective experience.

For example, if there is a car crash, everyone involved, including the people on the street nearby, will have a different perspective on what happened. Let's make up a fictional incident in order to explain what we mean. The person in the car that was traveling east will think that they got out into that intersection first. They believe, in their subjective experience, that they were the first to get into the intersection (it was a four-way stop), and thus, they had the right of way. They might describe it something like this:

"I pulled up to the stop sign, checked to see if anyone was around, and I slowly pulled out into the intersection. All of a sudden, that green car came out of nowhere, and slammed into the side of my car! They must not have been paying attention." However, when you ask the driver of the green car what happened, they say this: "I was sitting at the stop sign headed north on that same intersection, and I was sitting there for a long time. It was long enough for anyone to be able to see me. When the guy heading east came up, I assumed that he saw me, because I waited and waited. He didn't use a blinker, and I assumed that it was safe to pull out into the intersection. I hit his car because he pulled out right in front of me!" Then, let's ask the bystander what they saw. The bystander says, "I was watching the whole time. Neither of them stopped for the stop signs, they didn't even slow down!"

This fictional situation demonstrates the difference in subjective experience. We all experience phenomena differently. Even if we are looking at the same event or thing, each person will have a different experience of what actually happened, and each person will have a different perspective on what matters and how things appeared. Subjective experience, to a certain extent, is unexplainable. It is one of the great mysteries of our existence. How can we all exist on the same plane in one sense, while perceiving things so differently in our subjective experience? NLP recognizes this, and it remains the study of the subjective experience. Another definition for NLP is that it is the study of the structure of your subjective experience, the art, and science of communication, and the manual for your brain. Yet another example of a definition for NLP is the art and science of personal excellence. With Art, everyone brings out their unique personality and style to what they do and this can never be captured in words or techniques. It is science because there are a method and process for discovering the patterns used by outstanding individuals in any field to achieve outstanding results.

In 1979, Richard Bandler and John Grinder published a book called Frogs into Princes. This book argued that great psychotherapists acted on the basis of theory, which contributed to their effectiveness and enabled rapport with clients. They gathered information on the prominent psychotherapists at the time, and they noticed that they were all using certain principles and methods that lined up quite nicely together. They hypothesized that these principles could be used as an overall guide for working towards a change, and this made up the basis of their conception of NLP. NLP was the common factors in all different schools of psychology.

There are some main tenets of the theoretical basis for NLP. They will be listed below.

1.   Experience has a structure. This just means that when we incorporate the experience into our psyche, it has a way of being there. There are patterns that we make up to incorporate our

experiences and they are observable. For example, when we are kids and we have a fall that results in a scratched knee, we start to recognize that experience as something to be avoided, but also something that we experienced and were able to get over and recover from.

2. The map is not the territory. Different people have different patterns and ways of making up their mind about things. Different people will be looking at the same scenario and coming up with different observations about that scenario.

3. The mind and body are one system. Throughout history, there have been many different ways that this has been thought about. Early on, thinkers postulated that the mind was much more important than the body. In recent centuries, the body has become known to be as important as the mind in receiving information from the world and integrating our experiences.

4. People work perfectly. This means that people are effective at getting particular results. This doesn't mean that people are good at producing the best or healthiest outcomes for themselves, but rather that they are able to produce the same outcomes for patterns over and over again.

5. Individuals have all the resources that they need. This means that people have a vast reservoir of abilities. Rather than thinking about people at the surface level, you should think about what lay deep inside; people have a vast untapped amount of resources within them. Each time they have tried to solve a problem, or needed to figure something out, they add to their abilities.

6. There is no failure, only feedback. This saying means that failure is not something to think about as negative. Failure is just feedback. Failure will tell you what you need to do differently.

7. If what you're doing is not working, try something else. We constantly need to be checking in with our life strategies to see what is working and what we are doing right. If there is something that is not working, it needs to be changed. If there is something that is not working, it is okay to change it! Be flexible and adaptive.

"The Map is Not the Territory" is a common theme in NLP. By the territory, they mean the world. The world is objective, unchanging, and measurable. It is always there. The world is something that we can go check on. We can send out surveyors to see where state lines end and begin, and we can measure the depths of a lake, a river, and so on. It consists of measurable things that we can rest our hats on. The map is something that we all create for ourselves. The map in each of our minds is something that we have constructed in order to synthesize something out of our history, our experiences, and our cultural context. The maps that each person creates is limited and distorted through their past experiences and cultural context. Applied to behavioral change, the therapist's task is to understand and then work using the client's map to help them navigate a passage, both expanding their awareness and helping them journey from their condition to a more productive space.

The maps that people make of their world are represented by five senses: visual, kinesthetic (tactile), auditory, olfactory, and gustatory. Each experience in the world informs the continual development of the map. Bandler and Grinder suggested that each of us processes the majority of the information using one primary representational system. They maintained that the best therapist matched the patient's primary representational system. So how does this fit into Dark Persuasion? To talk about that, we must first acknowledge Dark Psychology. Dark Psychology is like the underside, the opposite of Positive Psychology. Positive psychology was created in the 1970s, by people looking to help others achieve an easier lifestyle by focusing on positives and solutions. Positive Psychology is focused on trying to bring positive energy into people's lives by centering their attention on the best parts of themselves. PP was coming out of an era of sustained optimism and successfulness. It was an era, after the World Wars, where people felt that they had everything at the tips of their fingers, that the world was sustainable and prosperous.

Fast forward to 2019. People aren't feeling so prosperous anymore, and people are starting to understand the depths of manipulation that surrounds them. People aren't feeling so positive and optimistic. Dark Psychology is the study of how people use manipulation, persuasion, and unethical principles to affect other people and get them to do their bidding.

Dark Persuasion

Dark Persuasion is a branch of Dark Psychology, and it is something that is very effective in its own way. Dark Persuasion is something that is used often. What are the principles of Dark Persuasion? The first is Brainwashing

Brainwashing is the practice of taking over someone else's capacity to think. Naturally, we all have unique thinking patterns and we all have the power to think critically about what is going on around us. Brainwashing takes away this power, and it puts that power into the hands of whoever is doing the brainwashing. Cults use this technique heavily, as it allows them to recruit and retain members. Brainwashing has many different implementations, but the principle remains the same throughout. A person is first brought into the fold of the new scenario. They are told that they matter, that they are worthy, and that they have a place to be in the new milieu. They must be separated from outside society in order to do this. The brainwashed person is convinced that this new way of thinking is a way to live better and happier. There is often a person who is the center of the brainwashing who is centered as very wise or smart. This person will be the "leader" of the cult, so to speak, and the person who is being brainwashed will start to think of this person as their new family director, so to speak.

This is all part of the breaking down of the self. In order to make sure that the person adapts and accepts this new milieu, their sense of self must be broken down. In the case of cults, this will often already have happened when the person joins. Cults look for people who are weekend by loneliness, suffering, or isolation. When a person has a good sense of self, they are less susceptive o being brainwashed. Thus, this must be attacked and broken down in order for a person to convince that this new way of living is the best.

Brainwashing might also employ guilt as a way to convince a person that they are in the best environment. Brainwashing will have people feeling guilty about their "past lives", and they will be presented with a solution for their guilt. Guilt and shame are very powerful emotions, and people will do whatever they think will work to get away from these emotions. Guilt and shame are what people feel when they are sad and ashamed about themselves. These negative emotions are what drive people to search out a solution, and often the solution can be manipulated by others in the form of brainwashing.

The brainwashers present the possibility of salvation. The possibility of salvation comes in the form of accepting the new ideas or format of the brainwashers. It comes in the form of accepting that they can be saved by this new person or group. Leniency is presented to the person. Rather than being told that their past transgressions are something that they will never be able to escape, they are told that they are able to escape it if they reach their new goals with the brainwashing. This, obviously, feels good, and it is hard to turn away from the possibility of salvation.

Another form of persuasion is hypnosis. Hypnosis works on a few basic principles. The first is the induction. Induction is where a person is helped along to a state of suggestibility, or relaxation. This is a state wherein they are put at ease and they are made vulnerable to messaging. The person who is being hypnotized is welcomed into this vulnerable state, and it is from there when they can be persuaded. After a person is put through an induction, their defenses are broken down, and they are able to receive suggestions. The suggestions may come in many different formats.

Some people seek out hypnosis to bring themselves away from bad habits, like smoking or other addictive habits. In this format, the person would go through the initial process of induction, and then, they hypnotist will make suggestions to them about how to quit smoking and messages relating to why they shouldn't smoke anymore. The hypnotist's suggestion in this formula will include statements like "You don't need to smoke. You don't have cravings. You don't have the social need to do it. You don't feel pressured to do it.", and so on. The suggestion can be in any direction, and there are very subtle ways in which a person can be suggested towards any goals. A hypnotist might use positive messaging, that might include positive feelings about the person's self or the world.

There is the military application of this process, which is fairly well-known. Initially, the soon-to-be-soldiers enter boot camp with their heads still in the mode of being back at home. Their goals are not formulated yet, and they are used to the comforts and privacy of home. They must be broken down first in order to be able to accept the messaging of the military. They enter boot camp and they are put through rigorous physical training and emotional damage. Their first experience in the boot camp is that everything is crazy and uncontrolled. They are given the message that they are powerless and that everything is against them, except their fellow soldiers. They are thrust into a world that is pure chaos and evil. They are told that nothing will save them, that nothing matters except to achieve whatever goal they must work on in that very moment. This is the way that they are broken down: they must learn that they are worth nothing, that they are empty, and not valid. Then, of course, they are built back up. This is the classic formula of brainwashing and hypnosis. The first phase works as the breaking down, or the induction, of the mind. This is where people are put into a state of suggestibility. Then comes the possibility of salvation. In the military case, what will save them is working hard and being tough, as well as bonding and working cohesively with their colleagues. The fellow soldiers, as well as the commanding officers, are the family and only friends of the soldiers. They are taught that they are worth less than dirt unless they are work-in toward a common goal with their fellow soldiers.

What this does is ultimately create a very cohesive, well-working unit of people, who believe that they are only able to function in this environment. They know that they can do because they are forced to be in such a terrible environment and they made it out alive. They were able to get through these terrible conditions because they were able to rely on one another for help, and the commanding officers gave them a rest at the end of their terrible exercises. This is a great illustration of Dark Psychology at work; the military can be known as an institution that has these principles nailed down to a well-oiled machine of science and psychology.

Resisting Dark Persuasion with NLP

These strategies are often used, by marketing companies, governmental units, and in interpersonal relationships, to manipulate you and make you act a certain way. NLP can help you resist these attempts.

NLP is a way of working that will help you to realize your way of thinking about the world, and engage with that to make changes. Remember, the map is different from the world. The world remains the same, but each person has a different map of it. NLP is all about finding how you present yourself with your map of the world.

For example, people develop different coping strategies based on what they have experienced in the past and how they got through it. There can be many ways of coping; some are what is called "adaptive" and some are what is called "maladaptive". Some are a mix of adaptive and maladaptive methods. Adaptive methods of coping are when a person finds ways to get through challenges that are healthy and propel the person closer to their authentic self. Maladaptive coping mechanisms are coping strategies, which draw people away from their authentic self and are more unhealthy ways to get by. One example of an adaptive coping mechanism is creating a support structure. Let's say that a person has a good job, and then suddenly, they are laid off. This presents a challenge to the person: they must find a new job where they can get paid and do work which fits them. An example of an adaptive coping mechanism would be if this person reaches out to friends, family, and acquaintances for help. This is a strategy that the person has employed that will help them to build connections. An example of a maladaptive coping mechanism would be if this person depends on drugs to get them through this difficult time. The reason that this is maladaptive is that it will help them in the short term, by taking away the feelings of sadness or frustration that comes along with the situation. However, they start to build a dependence on drugs for treating their feelings, and eventually, they will have to find other ways to cope, as the drug use becomes unsustainable.

NLP is all about analyzing your past coping mechanisms and other patterns and being able to work in that context. You can only work in the context that works for you; if you try to use other people's strategies for dealing with challenges, you will find that you can't quite make it work.

NLP is the study of how language is connected to mental programming. Each of us tells a story when we talk. We have developed our own individualized language, which is what we created from our experiences as a person. Creating our own way of communication is one of the most unique parts of humans.

People have a language all to themselves. It is the way in which they use the English language or whichever language it is they speak. When one person says a word, they might mean something completely different than another person. This can be seen in regional differences. People in the northern United States have certain patterns of speaking and people in the southern United States have another completely different pattern of speaking. Then, beyond that, there are cultural differences. In certain cultures, people speak less directly about things. Certain phrases are learned to be sued to refer to a specific phenomenon. Learning to communicate clearly can be useful, but it is also very important to learn how to communicate within the milieu of differing cultures and different people's perspectives. You must learn how to analyze someone's speaking patterns in order to benefit from NLP.

This is a big part of NLP: creating a road map of a person's language. It is by using their own language that you can change their mind, or realize when you are being persuaded. Think about a teacher who is coming into a class of kids for the first time. At first, they seem like a formal adult who is not "cool". However, if they learn to adapt to the kids' language, they are much more accepted. An adult who is very rigid in their language will not be as effective as a teacher who is able to pinpoint some of the key phrases in another person's language.

Humans tend to talk in stories. This is a key part of communication for nearly every person. People use stories to tell the world about what is happening. In fact, it is very rare that a person does not speak in stories. This is the way that we communicate and it's the way that we make understanding and meaning in the world. Telling stories is a very important part of NLP. In order to use NLP, you must be able to analyze and accept stories.

Let's think about this context for a moment. We'll use an example of an older woman, let's say about 65, who is telling you about her politics. You ask, "Why do you support Candidate X?" She tells you "Well, back in my day, people had to work hard to support themselves, and we didn't have anything handed to us. We worked hard, we lived through hard times, and we were able to get by and create something out of nothing."

Let's analyze what she said. She didn't provide you with any concrete answer, but she provided you with a lot of information. The story is what takes place of any specific points about Candidate X. This woman has a life story that she just let you a little bit in on. You can see how the story serves as the driver for the communication, rather than the specific information.

If you were to attempt to change this woman's mind, you would have to engage with her story. Her story is a common one. It is a story that older people often have. They tell that story of changing values and changing times. When they were younger, things were different, they say. They tell you about how when they were young, people had to work very hard to accomplish things that people don't have as much work to do with these days. This story may be true for them, but that doesn't mean that it is true for everyone else. That doesn't matter. In order to persuade or engage with NLP, you will have to accept the story.

This is one of the main components of NLP: acceptance. Persuasion has a lot to do with the person feeling like they are being heard, understood, and accepted. Acceptance will make a person feel safe, and when a person feels safe, they are more likely to agree with you. Accepting and validating a person's story is the first step to being able to influence them and persuade them. If you have the chance, you should dive deeper into the story.

How would you dive deeper into this woman's story? You would bring out some of the details. Where did you grow up? What did the breadwinner of your family do for work? They might have certain associations with certain types of work. Older people will sometimes no understand the complexities of modern occupations. You can think about some of the jobs that are part of the modern economy with technological companies. There are people who work for YouTube, for example, who work solely in the field of coordinating services with online companies who provide entertainment and television programs and integrate them with Youtube's services. This is something that you can probably get a general idea of, but for this older woman, this doesn't make sense. She doesn't understand what YouTube really does, let alone with the integration of services like this means. This is part of the intergenerational gap that we are talking about. In order to understand her and her story, you will have to engage with her on her level. You will have to learn how to use her language, and you can't expect her to know what you are talking about when you are talking in the vernacular of your current, modern-day situation. First, you must try to lean into the story and learn what her roadmap of the world looks like. You both live in the same world, but she will have a drastically different view of the world.

Let's use another example, this time with a very young person. Let's say they are 13 years old. Imagine the type of technology that they grew up with and they feel is natural. This will be completely different from what you grew up with. The world of technology is moving so quickly that new languages and new ways of communication are constantly evolving. This young person might have adapted to several turns of phrase and styles of communication that to you might seem very foreign.

In order to convince them, you will have to understand a little bit about their world. You would have to look into what kinds of entertainment they like if they are into sports, or music, or whatever else is relevant to that person's world. The way that a 13-year-old in this age communicates will be very different than that of a 65-year-old. They are both living in the same world, but they have completely different maps.

This subjectivity is the basis for NLP. When you realize another person's subjectivity, you are able to get inside their world. This is what the best psychotherapists do. They are able to look into a person's psyche and begin to analyze what is going on. This takes time, and many psychotherapists will require at least a few visits before they can ensure that they can work with surety and efficiency. A person will start to show their patterns after a certain amount of time. Patterns are not something that you can take hold of right away; it takes time to see how the person reacts in different circumstances and you can start to see where they have strengths and weaknesses.

Using NLP to Strengthen the Psyche

NLP is based on the techniques of psychotherapists. If you are able to engage yourself in these techniques, you will be able to work with yourself in a way that is similar to a therapist. You will, in essence, be able to become your own therapist. This is a very useful method to be able to strengthen your psyche and avoid being manipulated. You can use similar methods that a therapist might use to help reframe your thought process and analyze yourself.

There are many styles of psychotherapy, and as you try and apply the methods of NLP to yourself, it might be useful to know about the different approaches so that you can have some context for your work.

Sigmund Freud created psychoanalysis in the early 20th century. Freud used free association, dream analysis, and Rorschach tests to explore the subconscious of his clients. The classic picture that we have of an early therapist- the client laying back on a couch, talking, while another person observes and takes notes – this comes from psychoanalysis. This can be useful if you feel that you need to explore the subconscious. Exploring the subconscious is necessary if you feel that you have blocks in your path that you need to navigate. Many people will find that when they try and explore their subconscious, they are surprised at what they find. Psychoanalysis is all about being nonjudgmental and accepting whatever comes up. You can look for significance in the small things – little symbols that come up, memories, phrases, whatever it is. Each of these has a meaning that you can find if you delve deeper. A mind is a deep place and the subconscious has much to offer if you dive in.

Another school of psychology is the humanistic school. This developed out of the need to add a more personable element to psychology. This is where the therapist actually started supporting clients rather than being an impartial observer. In humanism, the therapist started employing the technique of perpetual acceptance. This means that no matter how crazy seeming or harsh was the subject that the client was talking about, the therapist just accepted it. They didn't pass judgment or react in any special way. This made it so people started to realize that they had someone to talk to who would accept their deepest and darkest secrets.

Behaviorism is another major school of psychology. It has been codified into the record books as one of the most important schools of psychology, for the way that it looks at behavior through an objective lens. In behaviorism, people are expected only to draw conclusions from what they can actually observe. When you are able to observe behavior that can be counted as real empirical evidence.

When you are going through the techniques of NLP and attempting to apply them to your life, you should choose one of these approaches. The first approach is more appropriate if you are looking to unearth deep and subconscious secrets and habits of yours. The second approach is good if you are a person who needs more support through the process. The third approach is good if you want to stay scientific and rational throughout the process.

Persuasion in the Social Media Age

An increasing amount of attention and connection that is available to the average person has marked the social media age. Back in the late nineties, a person would create a website for themselves or for their business through traditional methods, and the technology was much less ubiquitous than it is now. A person who wanted a whole web page devoted to themselves was going to have to work to achieve that and hire people to create a website. Now, every single person can have his or her own webpage, hosted on a social media site. This becomes their website, their journal, their business page.

This is a radical shift from the beginning days of the Internet when the website was scarce, and you had to find the stuff that you liked. Now, there are a few major corporations that run the social media sites and the provide pages to everyone that wants one. These companies have worked to integrate their websites with mobile smartphones and computers so that the user can experience these websites from their mode and per a part of the action.

A few social media sites are the ones that everyone uses. So, there is pressure for you to participate in social media. Most people do it, so when a person doesn't participate in social media, it is considered strange or out of place. Social media has become the way that we share our world with others, and tell stories. There are many viral videos and pieces of content that are shared instantly thought-out the world, and this is the power of social media. It is a place where ideas can light a fire and spread through the world in a moment's notice.

However, what is the dark side of social media? It has created a world of covert emotional manipulation and dark persuasion, and it has created huge blocks to us actually understanding when these tactics are being used against us.

When you are present with someone, you are able to look at their face and involve yourself in a constant feedback loop with them, and you perceive their body language, and you get a real sense of what the person is like and what they are conveying to you. Text is much more limited. Text is how we communicate a lot these days, whether it is posted on social media or just text messages to friends. Text is not the same as being with a person. Digital text is even less powerful communication than a phone call because at least with a phone call you can hear the person's voice, which is a great expression. With text communication, however, you only get whatever a person is able to write down.

This makes social media a perfect platform for persuasion and manipulation. People can make themselves seem like they have whatever characteristics that they want. They can make themselves seem pious, cool, concerned, justice-oriented, tough, or any other number of attributes. Businesses that are not legitimate can make themselves seem totally successful and real.

Scams are easy to pull on the internet, especially on Facebook, Instagram, and Twitter.

The social media age has made us more afraid of being ourselves. We want to put on a certain image to the world that says the message that we think we want to be perceived as. This could be that you are cool, smart, or popular. Most people want to be portrayed as attractive and successful on social media. It is the age of FOMO or fear of missing out, and that is reflected in our behavior. The fear of missing out is the feeling that people describe when they perceive that people are having fun somewhere because of their online posts. People see the posts and think that this person has the life that they want. They feel that they are not good enough to have the type of interesting experiences that these people have, and it makes us feel bad to be ourselves and raises all sort so of issues with anxiety and coping. Sometimes a person has the habit of separating himself or herself from whatever situation they are in by using their phone in the company of others. This makes them disconnected, and instead of truly being with the people they are with; they start to never really get a connection, and they stay to themselves. This can disrupt relationships because this person is always wanting to set something up in the future or thinking about past events, and they never spend their time in the present. This is what social media does; it takes you away from the present. It is a way to escape, and American life has always been about escapism.

There is some main pathology that seems to come from our current social media landscape, and one of the main incidences seems to be anxiety. Anxiety is a natural feeling that humans encounter. It comes from the evolutionary need to protect us from the environment and form tether humans and animals. Back when people lived just before and during the hunter-gatherer phase, people had to protect themselves from the wild and unpredictable forces of nature. We don't have to live like that anymore, but these anxiety impulses are still within us. This has affected the human race since the dawn of the industrial age.

Anxiety makes us more vulnerable to manipulation and persuasion because it makes us think that we are missing something. It creates the illusion that other people have something that we want. They are able to engage us very directly, without having to go through any of the traditional channels.

When the industrial age began, humans started to become disconnected format the things that they use to make, the foods they ate, and the things that they needed to survive. Before this happened, the creation of goods was centralized, and led to a completely different landscape of how we got along in the world. This was before we were able to mass-produce items and it was before we were able to make things on the incredible scale that we are now. The industrial revolution completely transformed the lives of humans in the West. Rather than being responsible for making things and feeling in touch with the land, humans now were subjected to cruel working hours, and productivity took over as the main value of the land. Before this, people spent time with the goods that they had and the food that they ate. People were responsible for making things for themselves and master tools in the process. The mastering of physical tools lends itself to the mastery of metaphysical tools. This disconnection can be seen now.

This disconnection between what we eat, what we use, what we do, and who we are has caused all kinds of problems in our society. We don't grow our own food; we buy it from the store. We have never met the animal that we eat every time we buy meat. The animals live far away, and the process of butchering them is not our problem. This goes the same for other products and foods. Those tomatoes you are eating had to be picked by someone; they had to be picked and grown and taken care of. We don't do that stuff anymore, and what this has led to is anxiety.

Anxiety is produced when we don't feel that we have power, and we feel that we don't know what to do. Anxiety is, to a certain extent, a natural phenomenon in humans and animals; it provides us with a safety mechanism that springs forth our fight or flight response in order to protect ourselves. In this way, anxiety is important and good. However, many people now have an imbalance in their anxiety, and they have little reason to be afraid. However, they still feel anxious, and the level of threat that their body is telling their mind is there is really not there. This affects our interactions, our relationships, our ability to relax, and every other part of human everyday functioning. It makes us nervous, and there might be thought content that goes along with it. Worry and anxiety are closely related, but they are not the same thing. Worry is more about the thought content that comes along with anxiety. Anxiety is the physical feeling, and the worry is the thought content that you are focusing on.

What is the main thing that is missing? Real connection. This is what social media uproots. Real connections with the world are important for almost everyone in the world. While there are some parts of social media that actually do let us connect more to the world and to others, there are many aspects of it that leave us feeling disconnected and fail to ever increase our level of connection with the world. The real connection makes it so that you start to learn what actually can be trusted in the world rather than having to trust whatever shows up on your computer screen and offers you money.

However, it's not about the technology itself. It's about how we use technology. You can use a flower vase to display flowers or bash someone over the head. If someone is using Facebook to connect with relatives that live far anyway and they are not to visit much anymore, then that is great. In this case, social media has been able to foster a connection between families that were inconvenient or impossible before. This is great, and it is not the technology that made that happen, it was the person. However, if a person is obsessed with looking at pictures of their peers, while feeling insecure about themselves, and always checking in with their phones and never being in the present moment, then they are not using the technology well, and they will have to learn to change their behavior if they want to feel better.

Some people are able to use social media for their advantage, and others are not. Some people may find themselves wrapped up in what they read and see online and they will start to question their own lives. They will start to feel that they are empty, or that their lives are boring, or not as interesting as other peoples'. This is because they are not getting enough real human connection in their lives. It is sad to see, and the paradoxical nature of this phenomenon is such that when craven people are trying to portray themselves to look good on social media, those who can see through it are broadcast these images. Instead of looking good or cool, they are broadcasting their insecurities to the world.

Which, actually, doesn't sound like a bad thing. Broadcasting your insecurities to the world is something that a confident person would do. That is something that a person who doesn't give a crap about what other people thinks of them. However, there is the problem of intention. When people are making posts, they are not aware of what is going on. They are just completing the cycles in their mind. They get a dopamine hit every time they post something or get likes a post. It has a built-in reward system, and social media websites are designed to draw people in and get others ever engaged with the site.

The Smartphone has become a big problem with people on how to deal with problems of anxiety. The phone is something that we all carry around, in our pockets, in our hands, in our bras; we carry them everywhere, and no matter what we are doing, the phone has to be nearby. There are some great technological advances that have been made because of this product, and there are incredible implications for the good that the smartphone can do in the world.

However, many people are not so good at moderating their behavior when it comes to cell phones and smartphones, and they get addicted. It becomes basically a little computer that we carry around, which is capable of playing TV shows, radio, all kinds of media, as well as performing countless tasks. It can connect you to any page on the Internet. You can take a picture wherever you go.

There are so many functions that this contributes greatly to our addictions. Our addiction to the phone is always on the borderline between pathology and helpful; each person will have to learn where their lines are. A person who uses their phone too much might just have to learn to slow down a bit and be more mindful now. Some people are not really able to have a good time with friends when they're hanging out, just because they are checking their phone all the time. It is a compulsive thing that they do, and it is to feel connected. Really, they are just being manipulated. They are being manipulated by the companies that run these sites, and by other people who have fallen under the spell of social media.

Learn To Analyze Friends, Coworkers, Lovers

Learning to apply psychology to friends, coworkers, and lovers is primarily a matter of boundaries. Each person might have different interests in their possible angle of manipulation. Each of us plays different roles in our lives. In one role, we are called to be a family member. This might refer to your given or born family, or it might refer to your chosen family. "Chosen family" refers to the people you include in your life to the closest degree. This might include friends or other people to which you have chosen to be closest. Coworkers include people who we are often required to be around. Some lucky people get to choose who they work with, but most of us are required to work with people at random. Friends are a category of people who we choose to spend our time with, mostly doing enjoyable activities. Lastly, lovers include those with whom we choose to be romantic.

For the first category, friends, we must establish the types of boundaries which we want to have when dealing with friends. Friendships should be the type of relationships that bolster your health as an overall person. Friends are people you choose to spend time with, and hopefully, you don't choose to spend time with people who are not good for you. Often, there is a mix of positives and negatives in a friendship. You might have a friend who is annoying sometimes, but at other times, you have great fun and close connection with. It is all about maintaining that balance. Friendships can become toxic if a person is using someone else, being selfish, or not establishing a connection. Friendships should be a place of solace and connection, but you also have the right to challenge friends. You have the right to push them to be better, and you should be able to tolerate them calling you out on your negative qualities, as well. Friendships are all about balance. A good friendship is a partnership that includes connection and positive energy.

Coworkers are a little trickier because these are not people we choose. They are mostly people we are assigned to spend time with. Some people have trouble separating their work life and their friend life, and they will have trouble acting professionally around people they like. They might try to make things too personal at work, and they will not be able to create the type of relationship that is appropriate for work conditions. A person must have a solid support system outside of the workplace in order to have a balanced work life. Having a good relationship with coworkers means that you are able to be pleasant and nice and effective in the workplace, while not asking too much of people about the intimate details of their lives. Sometimes (perhaps more often than we'd like), we have coworkers who we don't like at all. In this situation, you can let go of the possibility of being friends at all. This is okay! You can't be friends with everyone. Coworkers who we don't like are a great opportunity to grow as a person. This is a challenge for you. Will you be able to work effectively with this person, even if you don't like them? This will include the challenge of detachment. You have to tell yourself that even if this person is someone with which you don't want to spend time, you have to. This gives you the requirements to work with. You have to spend at least 20 hours a week interacting with Frank. Frank is a cranky person who doesn't know how to laugh or have fun. Even though you are not like this, you must, to a certain extent, match Frank's mood at the moment. You must become a little more detached and less fun-loving than you usually are. In the workplace, you must learn to accommodate Frank's rigidity and bad mood. Now, this goes both ways, and Frank must learn to be at least partially pleasant so that he is able to have a job and work with people. However, if you learn to work with people that you don't like, you will have learned a great skill. Some boundary issues in this context with our example character Frank might be that you learn not to try to engage Frank in conversation outside of work matters. When you are with him, it's all about work. Adjustments like this have to be made. You have to just know that you are only going to get so far in the conversation and go from there. You must just learn to say, "This person is this way, and there is no changing that."

Now, there are often other challenges in the workplace. Sometimes, people are too friendly. These are times in which you must learn to remind yourself of the purpose of the day: to get work done effectively. You can learn to draw boundaries in this arena as well. These might include cutting a conversation short and learning how to "cut people off" as they start to ramble. These boundaries might also include not sharing information about yourself. You must learn that this is okay! It doesn't mean that you are shutting yourself off from the world. It just means that you have a good sense of boundaries.

Family is yet another category of people with whom we must figure out our relationships. In some cases, a relationship with family members is not possible or necessary. This happens in cases where people are separated from their family for whatever reason. For people who grew up with abusive parents, it can be healthy to cut out traditional family members and grow a new chosen family outside of them. However, for many people, family connections are deep and important. It connects us to our humanity and reminds us of where we come from. Parents should help nurture and grow their children, and we should be grateful for this if our parents did a good job. At a certain point in development, we are able to relate to our parents as simply people rather than a mom and dad. There are some boundaries in this area too. Some people have parents who are very expecting and controlling and might feel the need to draw boundaries where the parents are and aren't allowed to see or comment on their lives.

This goes for other family members as well, like siblings and extended families. Again, it is all about striking a balance.

Once you have firmly established the different roles for people in your life, you can start analyzing whether or not the relationships are equitable. You might find that someone has set up the relationship to be more beneficial for them than for you. You might find that you are manipulating someone else!

Chapter 2: Covert Manipulation

When talking about manipulation, it is useful to frame things in the context of a leader and followers. Leaders can do whatever they want with the power that they have, but they can't do anything without being able to control followers. This is manipulation.

Understanding How the Mind Works

The human mind is unlike anything else. It is a control center receiving signals from nerves, body parts, muscles, tendons, organs, and automatically processing the appropriate responses, learning, and growing. The mind is an impossible place to understand. Many disagree about what the mind is.

The Materialists, for example, would argue that nothing exists outside of the brain. There is an atheist, science-centered viewpoint that postulates that there exists nothing outside of the physical, real material of the world, like our bodies and observable things like the sun, earth, other people, etc. They say that there is not consciousness floating somewhere in an aura-like haze around a person and that the experience of consciousness is a product of the brain. The mind for the Materialists is the human experience of the brain working and directing our bodies.

Others point to a soul and minds that is altogether a different metaphysical existence than the brain. The brain and body exist in a real material world, where the mind and soul exist in a real non-material one. This argument of duality manifests in all kinds of forms in the arguments about what we are and what our consciousness is.

One thing that we can establish for sure is that we exist. Don't get caught up in all that talk about a simulation. Sure, that is a useful analogy for consciousness, but to actually believe that we are a brain in a vat? Well, you would have to adjust to that reality. Moreover, it might actually not be so different from your goals and aspirations anyway. Because even if it is all a simulation, there is not Matrix-style way to break out of it, that we know of. People have tried all kinds of drugs and explored the consciousness that way. Spiritual experiences are reported to be ways that we can break out of this reality. However, for most people, we will perpetually be living in this reality. There is no easy long-term escape.

There is one "healthy" alternative: mindfulness and meditation. Mindfulness occurs when you are paying attention to the body and only the experience you are having at the moment. Practicing mindfulness can help people to escape the mind, to have an opportunity to look in rather than out, and to realize important thoughts about themselves.

The mind, first and foremost, is resultant to our experience. If we are fed with education and learning at a young age, this will influence how we develop. Context is everything. Cultural traditions, language, and all kinds of other difference shape the diversity in our minds. There is, however, a common thread: human consciousness.

The mind is always changing. We absorb the factors around us like a sponge. Any of the information that enters through the five senses may make its way to the unconscious or the conscious memory. Each little experience is encoded somewhere in the brain, or determined not important enough to keep. The human being is a sensory animal who has evolved to be able to detect others and itself, see, hear, and smell predators, to enjoy and be disgusted by foods, along with countless other functions.

Our sensory input is how we experience the world. If you are talking about the "brain in a vat", then the sensory input is all the information that a person would need. It is through this filter that we find our way in the world.

One side of the argument says that we should be wary of the info that we get through our senses. There are several perspectives on this. Firstly, when we dream, most of us are completely tricked into thinking that the dream is reality. It is only when we wake me that we find that our bodies are still lying in our beds and that none of this has happened. But when we are in dreams, our dreams are our reality. There is no way to say that what you experience in a dream isn't real. It's real. It may not be real to anyone else in the universe at that particular second, but it is still real to you at that moment.

Now, some people have reportedly developed the skill of becoming aware when they re dreaming. This is an interesting skill that has been widely reported as possible. However, the main point remains: that the sensory input of dreams is very convincing, and it is one area that points to the fallibility of our senses. Most of the time, they are pretty trustworthy, or so it seems. When you see something that you are going to walk into and you walk into it and feel the pain as it bumps against your head, you are experiencing the true-ness of your senses. You sensed in your vision something that blocked your path, and you have evidence, the pain, that your vision was the reality.

Another perspective is about how illusory real stimuli can be. People can make paintings that, when viewed from a certain angle, create the illusion of a hole in the ground of skew of perspective. Visual illusions are present everywhere from art to the atmosphere to visual lines in the distance.

Another factor is emotion. You never know when emotions are affecting a person's perception. The level of intensity of some emotions can be incredible, and it can cause a drastic change in perception in a person.

So we have to take a mediated stance on where or not to trust the senses. We must acknowledge that they can be tricky and that the senses will often mislead us. The mind can also be a predictable thing; how many people do you know that do the same thing every day? We tend to have habits and lifestyles, and we generally stick to the way we liked to behave within that lifestyle. Habits and lifestyle are intertwined, and making changes to one can lead to changes in the other.

The way to start observing your own mind is to start identifying emotions. This may seem like an easy thing to do at first but it may be very challenging for some people. Emotions can be understood differently than feelings; feelings are a mental or cognitive process. This involves what you are thinking about. So, if you are thinking something, there will be word content associated with it. Sometimes this is known as self-talk. This could be taking many different forms, but it always has thought the content in word form, and this is what distinguishes feelings from emotions. Emotions are the purely physical state that makes up anger, anxiousness, sadness, grief, and all the other emotional states.

Emotions, then, rather than having thought content, are a physical state, that doesn't necessarily precipitate thought content, but often do. Sometimes an emotion will be experienced without words and will be expressed immediately. An example of this is a person feeling extremely angry, and in a split second, hitting someone else physically. We are not condoning this type of violence but it is an example of a person reacting to emotion without thought content and expressing their emotion.

The other side of this would be a person who can't express their emotions and rather gets all up in their head with it. This often happens with people who are depressed or anxious. Anxiety tends to have big effects on thought patterns and thoughts, in this case, will often turn to negative self-talk or worry. Worry is a huge byproduct of anxiety and they tend to go together. Identifying emotions, then, is the study of seeing what's going on within the body.

When children get to the age of being able to express emotions and identify them, they often lack the skill that it takes to be an adult and identify emotions. A child or an underdeveloped adult will not be able to describe their emotions naturally and accurately. They may mislabel certain situations or they may not have the words to describe how they feel. A child may describe their experience as "mixed-up" when in fact they were angry. Sometimes people will mistake sadness for anxiety.

It takes a while to develop the skills to accurately label and identify your emotions. There are many ways to do this. The ones we will talk about in this chapter are journaling, self-reflection, and art.

Each person will experience emotions differently and this is good and necessary. Some people will cry when they feel sad, others will rage. Some people are comfortable with some emotions more than others are. For example, someone might be comfortable being the angry person because this is where most of his or her experience lay. They have grown up around people who express their angry easily and they themselves express anger easily. When it comes to sadness, however, they have no idea of how to express or show it. They may even be ashamed to show their sadness. Some demographic groups tend to lean one way or the other.

Another method to redevelop emotional awareness is self-reflection. Again, you should try to do this however is comfortable for you. If you like to be in nature, visit your favorite nature –filled the place and have a moment in silence to think about a recent emotional state you have. You could also pay attention to your current emotional state, and ask yourself: "How am I feeling right now? Why am I feeling this way?" you can also explore the experiences that you had to lead up to your current emotional state, and from here, you can find strategies to increase or avoid those emotional states.

Yet another method is art. Art is a great way to use non-verbal expression to increase your mental well-being. Art is a magical carrier of emotion for humans; we tend to use art to understand the world and make sense of it. This is not the only function of art, however; there are many functions. One is dancing; others are relaxation, grief, mourning, celebration, and war-rousing. There are many functions of music, and nearly all of them our emotions. Music is a great example of an art form that can transform the emotional experience and bring about emotional awareness.

Leader Manipulation

For a leader, every resource has a constraint, and every constraint is potentially a resource. There is little that is easy and straightforward, and the leader who really lets things drift along has forfeited the title. The human condition is very complicated and very messy. To cope with it, one must simplify, and the simplifications should neat and logical. But in fact, they're very often neither, first because they may be arrived at under pressure when there is the urgent need to take action, and second because they are often the product not of disinterested logical thought but of a compromise between interests. So, the simplifications turn out to be messy and complicated like the reality from which they sprang.

Leadership, in one of its aspects, is the art of cutting into this chaos and imposing a simplified definition on the situation, that is, making people act as if the simplified picture were the reality. This cannot be done in an honest, open, reasoned, dispassionate, and scientific fashion. The leader must be partisan. He must use rhetoric. He must be ruthless, be ready to subvert values while appearing to support them, and be clever enough to move the discourse up to a level where opportunism can be successfully hidden behind a screen of sermonizing about the eternal verities. Leadership is a form of cultivating ignorance, of stopping doubts and stifling questions. Most leaders would reject this assertion about the requirements of their art. If their opponents do happen to behave in that way, it is not because such behavior is inevitable (they themselves never do such things!), but because of those particular people's lack virtue. Successful leadership requires conviction, transparent honesty, tenacity, and courage. It is astonishing how much patent falsehood there is in public life. This is an expression not of regret that people are dishonest but of surprise that politicians appear to get away with dishonesty so easily and so often. Is there not something strange about a culture such as ours that condemns lies but at the same time condones them with such categories as promise and rhetoric?

No less striking is the ready cynicism of the politicians themselves. A man who has divorced and remarried, who is widely believed to be quite uninterested in his children and grandchildren, and who rarely goes to church on Sundays presents himself and is apparently accepted as a great example of Christian family living. The same man lends his benign television presence to the opening of the "Special Olympics", having first done his utmost to cut financial aid for the handicapped. Another candidate issues a false report that her rival is to be indicted for the misuse of public money and does o on the eve of the election when there is no opportunity for a rebuttal. Of course, she may not have known that the report was false.

Leadership is the art of controlling followers it is presented as an art because to practice it successfully, one needs to have a talent. That is what is meant when a leader's intuitions are praised as evidence of divine guidance or condemned as the "devil's own luck". In more mundane terms a leader must have leadership quality, and leadership is too complicated or too subtle an activity to be reduced entirely to rules and procedures that could be taught in a classroom. That is what leaders say, and they are correct. At least they are correct if one is envisaging a definitive and exhaustive theory of leadership. Short of that logical perfection there are certainly known regularities in the way leaders behave in their efforts to control their followers. These can generally be known as covert manipulation.

Strategies available to a leader and appropriate for the task at hand depend on several different things. Strategies vary not only according to the disposition of followers but also according to their relationship with the leader.

Leadership belongs to a larger category, manipulation. Covert manipulation is the domination or the exercise of power. Domination is the capacity to make another person act in a particular way, whether or not that person wants to do it or whether or not they are aware of the domination. There are varieties of domination other than leadership. The master dominates the slave because he can use force. The employer dominates the worker because he pays him and can withhold payment or fire them. The official dominates lesser officials because both accept the latter's subordination as a right and proper in a bureaucratic organization. The king dominates his subjects for the same reason. Finally, in a different sense, the master of performing art – music, painting, literature, fashions, or certain sports. – dominates lesser artists in the field because they follow his or her example. This kind of artist dominates even if he is unaware of their existence.

A follower is a person that accepts guidance that may receive and takes the appropriate action. These two dimensions (obedience and action) sort out the good from the bad follower. But it is no simple matter to decide what positions on these dimensions represent good and bad. It depends on the context. This is always going to be complicated. A nonfollower is someone who takes initiatives on his or her own behalf. Such a person, wanting something, acts without being told what to do. There are societies that have no leaders because for most practical purposes every person is self-sufficient. The Hazda people of northern Tanzania have been described as having no chiefs, although occasional opportunists try to dominate them and exploit others. The Hazda are forest-dwelling hunters and gatherers who make a living easily and are more or less protected from outside pressures by the forest, by their lack of property, and by their ability to keep out of the way. They have little need of one another for mutual protection from outsiders, for the exploitation of material resources, or maintenance of the internal order. They share the game if the kill is big enough to share, but mostly they hunt alone. With certain dually enjoined exceptions, the sharing is quite casual, people coming to help themselves. They have small necessity to cooperate in solving problems and therefore they have no leaders.

This is not the world that we live in in the USA. It is interesting to learn about these cultures because they are far from how we live. There may very well still be interpersonal manipulation in this and other cultures like it, but there is no widespread, overall manipulation by governmental structures because they have no need for it. The government is the largest example of covert manipulation that we have. Cultures without a government or leaders exemplify that there, in fact, can exist a society without large-scale manipulation.

Societies vary widely in their views on leadership. In some, leadership itself is elevated. In others, it is belittled. Further, attitudes change as the context changes. In wartime, a leader is a hero. In peacetime, the leader might become an embarrassment. That was also Winston Churchill's fate. If the style of leadership that is value vary, then people's expectations constitute part of the context that explains why one style rather than another is effective. The expectations are themselves a function of values, beliefs, and customs. Values, beliefs, and customs together constitute culture.

Covert manipulation has a lot to do with the creation of the trust. Trust is a very complicated concept. It has an affinity to credit, which means the granting of services without insistence on an immediate return, in the confident expectation that the return will be forthcoming in due time. But trust is not quite the same. It includes an element that denies altogether the notion of a return or a reward. The relationship is intrinsic; it is its own reward. Trust also is generalized and divorced from the specification in a way that credit is not. Ideally, followers do not so much trust the leader to perform successfully this or that particular activity. They simply trust him or her as a person, and at that extreme, the relationship shades off into devotion or into love.

Leaders endeavor to create in the mass of their followers that nonspecific personal and direct form of trust which is akin to love and which prevents close and impartial scrutiny and accounting of their performance, while not being seen openly to do so. The leader claims a personal and direct moral relationship by two main rhetorical devises: the familial and the numinous. One cannot help feeling that charismatic forms-especially the numinous- are bizarre manifestations of leadership. Why do people accept another person, a human being like themselves, as a divinity, or a great leader? There must be particular contexts that make such behavior sensible.

So far in this chapter, we have mostly discussed what it is like to be subject to covert manipulation on a grand scale in the political context. So, what about the interpersonal context? People who are manipulative know how to push all the right buttons in order to affect your life. They know what you care about, they know how you operate, and they know how to get you emotional.

Interpersonal Manipulation

This happens a lot in relationships. Right now, one of the most common relationship dynamics is between the man who is afraid of emotional or other kinds of intimacy and the woman who is insecure. This is, of course, not the prevailing dynamic for all relationships, but people who are in the 20-35 demographic right now tend to have this dynamic more than others.

This dynamic is one of a person who is afraid of committing to others on one end and a person who is afraid to stand up for themselves on the other side. Let's start by discussing the person who is afraid of intimacy in this situation. The person who is afraid of intimacy was probably brought up to think that you can have anything you want in the world, as long as you work hard and you deserve it. If you are a good person, you can make your dreams a reality. This is different than in past generations. Past generations were told that you have to sacrifice of yourself to get work done and that you should create a family to further the country and your ancestors. They were raised in an economy where things were considered scarce. They were taught that there weren't that many possibilities for them in the world and that they needed to work hard to get by in the world, not for themselves, but for others. This is the type of thinking that has stuck with many of the older generations that are now still living among us. Of course, there is no viewpoint that is right or wrong, just intergenerational different.

This is different from the past twenty years or so of children, who were raised not in an economy of scarcity, but rather of abundance. They were told that you could do whatever you want, that you are special, and that you deserve whatever is allowed to you. The allure of hard work still exists, but no, people are more commonly oriented towards working for themselves rather than for a family.

This is all to give you some background information about the relationship dynamic that is common for millennials and the upcoming Gen Y. The person who was raised in this milieu is thinking that they should keep their options open, that they should be able to keep people at arm's length, and that they should be able to always be free to pursue what they want to pursue and do what they want to do. This is the way that Millennials operate as a status quo. This leads to problems in relationships; where the old guard had different problems relating to lack of intimacy because of lack of understanding, Millennials have problems with lack of intimacy due to fear. There is a fear among people that they will not be able to find what is perfect and good for them if they open themselves u. Rather than needing to start a family and find out what it takes to sacrifices something, they are always looking for a better and better situation. They might be looking for a better partner, a better job, a better opportunity here and there, rather than looking to find what works and actually committing to something. This leaves people in a lurch. This is one side of the relationship: fear of intimacy. The other side of that same relationship is insecurity. The insecure person is okay with their partner being afraid of and avoiding real intimacy because they have not accepted themselves as a person who is actually deserving of love and affection. They think of themselves as a person who is not quite as good as the rest of the world, and they think that they are not whole or deserving.

Thus, you put these two people together, and you have a common relationship dynamic among Millennials. This is often fraught with manipulation.

When the time comes to have a situation where there comes the choice of actual intimacy, the person who is afraid of intimacy will find some kind of excuse. This is a form of interpersonal covert manipulation. There might also be other demonstrations of covert manipulation.

Let's take the fictional example of Mike and Lena. Mike is a 23-year-old man who has graduated from college and is looking for a girlfriend to spend time with. Lena is a 25-year-old woman who has also graduated from college, works part-time as a photographer and part-time at a coffee shop. Mike and Lena meet due to a mutual friend, and they hit it off, learning that they both enjoy similar things. They start to meet up regularly and go on dates, going to shows, restaurants, and the rest. Mike is excited and wants to be in a relationship with Lena. Lena knows that she doesn't want to be in a relationship with Mike. However, she is so insecure that she doesn't want to face the reality of having to let go of Mike and tell her that she doesn't want to be in a relationship. Lena "leads him on", and keeps going on dates, because she doesn't want to feel alone in the world. This is covert manipulation. The reason that it is covert manipulation is that Lena is keeping her real desires secret. She thinks that if she is real with Mike, and tells him that she doesn't want a relationship, she will feel lonely and abandoned.

Lena keeps things going, and when Mike expresses his affection, she tells him that she feels the same way. It is true to a certain extent because Lena enjoys Mike's company and likes to spend time with him. However, Lena knows that Mike wants something committed, and she keeps spending time with him. A typical conversation in this dynamic might go something like this:

"I love hanging out. We should go to the mall tomorrow and go to that store you mentioned."

"Mmm, I like hanging out with you too. Tomorrow night sounds good, I'll just have to check and see what my work schedule looks like", responds Lena. However, in her mind, she is not thinking about having to check her work schedule. She is actually thinking about another man with whom she has some interest. This is covert manipulation; Lena is making him think that she only has reservations in hanging out because of her work schedule, but in reality, she is trying to meet up with someone else.

This is just one example. Let's think about another example. Mark is 32 and Sarah is 31. They are both young professionals in a mid-sized American city. They meet on a dating app and the first night that they meet up, they go out dancing and drinking and have a great time. They're enjoying each other's company and the excitement of being out on the town. They are loving being with each other and it feels exciting and new. Sarah doesn't do this as often as Mark does. They go home and make love together, their first night. Sarah stays the night. In the morning, Mark makes breakfast and Sarah starts to pack up and leave. They have breakfast, and Sarah sticks around. She is very excited, and she is picturing in her mind a loving relationship where Mark and she will be able to spend time in the future. Mark, however, is not on the same page. Mark has become addicted to "the game" and having fun in the wild nightlife scene of his city. Mark is good at the game, and he likes establishing these one-night stands. Mark knows that he doesn't like to go further in relationships after the first night, but he has trouble telling people this. He is not acting ethically here, because he makes Sarah feel like this will be an ongoing thing. He tells her how much he enjoyed their time and is physically affectionate.

Psychical affection is part of the manipulation here. Covert manipulation is not always just verbal language. It is often touch or sex. Mark knows that he is engaging in behavior that telegraphs his love in a certain way. He knows that when he is physically engaged in certain ways that it is sending the message that he wants to be in a committed relationship with the person. He also knows that he doesn't want to be in that relationship, but he engages in the behavior nonetheless. This is covert manipulation. It is especially sneaky because of the physical component. Mark feels guilty because deep down, he knows what he is doing. He knows that he must take it slow if he wants to actually establish a lasting relationship, but he doesn't do that because he is being driven by his animalistic tendencies.

In the first example, covert manipulation was being driven by fear. In this example with Mark, it is being driven by desire. Each is something that you might experience in interpersonal relationships. Each one is something that you will have to defend yourself against.

Propaganda

Let's switch gears for a moment and talk about propaganda and advertising. The techniques of propaganda and advertising are employed to influence the behavior of the masses. Propaganda and advertising are used to stimulate us to believe in something, to actively support someone, something, an idea perhaps, to buy a product, a service, to behave in a particular manner. Although the term propaganda has mostly fallen out of style, a close look at propaganda will indicate that it is simply a form of spreading information to indoctrinate an audience according to a plan.

Propaganda can take on many different forms and wear many faces. A public relations campaign sponsored by a state government in order to stimulate more tourism can be considered propaganda. Their goal is to attract new businesses and industry and increase investment within the state. This is designed to propagate the idea that the state has a great deal to offer. The campaign is also designed to instruct the public as to the advantages of this state over the other forty-nine states. The campaign is further designed to influence behavior. They want you to move here, to visit here, and to spend money here.

Much of the public suspicion regarding the term propaganda comes from its connection with political motives and movements. This is what can happen when the American public has heard propaganda used so often in connection with Communism. It has almost become synonymous with communism. However, this is not the point of propaganda. T can be used to promote a wide variety of concepts and ideas.

Many large companies use this technique in their advertising. In evaluating this propaganda technique as to its truthfulness and value, the reader must ask: is there really a connection; is there sufficient proof to establish the connection. Does this connection make someone's product any more desirable? What is the motive behind the company's statement? Another propaganda device that is closely related to the association is identification. An individual most often uses this technique in order to receive broader acceptance in the group he is trying to influence. The more they accept him, the greater will be the possibility of their accepting his ideas. A manager addressing a group of employees may remind them that he once worked within the ranks. A politician campaigning before an American Legion group may remind his audience that he is also a veteran and can thus better understand their concerns.

Identification is used to gain the trust and acceptance of the audience. You might want to review someone's comments in an attempt to spotlight the key phrases that would lead to identification. Remember that, despite the success or failure of the speaker or writer to gain audience acceptance, the ideas themselves will have to stand or fall on their own merits.

The propaganda technique known as the bandwagon technique is often associated with political campaigns and is aimed at creating the impression that "if you can't to be on the winning side, you'd better get behind our guy before it's too late." Since no one wants to be on the losing side, this can be very effective. The idea is to create the impression that there is a popular movement gaining momentum from growing popular support and acceptance.

It would be a mistake to limit the bandwagon approach to politics because it is very often used in advertising. The bandwagon technique is an obvious attempt to influence a person's behavior through an emotional appeal rather than through logical persuasion based on evidence and good judgment. It is rooted in the premise that the crowd can do your thinking for you, and thus negates the value of the personal opinion.

Bifurcation is a method used more and more these days by propaganda outlets. Hate, fear, and mistrust foster the division of people and nations into camps based on opposing points of view. Bifurcation can be devastating because it is based on the premise that there are only two sides to any problem. There is never gray, always black and white. It is ridiculous to suggest that there is never a gray area in any issue, and a wise person can always recognize that bifurcation indicates the extremes, and there is much room between the extremes for dozens of alternate points of view. It is certainly possible to be in favor of some federal help for parochial schools without being overwhelmingly in favor of

Uncle Sam's picking up the entire tab. This technique would be less dangerous if individuals would recognize the possibility of taking a stand somewhere in between the extremes.

Another deceptive method is the use of the testimonial in gaining acceptance of a product or idea. In this technique, the propagandist or advertising person uses some authority as an aid to selling an idea or product. The problem is that the authority is very often not an authority at all, but merely a well-known personality or public figure.

The use of favorable generalities (glittering gernetalitieso relies on words that trigger favorable response, words that imply positive attitudes. The propagandist who uses this technique hopes that the audience will overlook the fact that he supports his point of view with abstractions. He hopes that they will be convinced by the appeal itself and overlook the lack of evidence. These generalities are usually loaded with emotional content. If a person claims he is for "human rights' each person in the audience can apply his own stand on human rights and then equate that with the propagandist's view s on the same subject.

Chapter 3: Persuasion and Defense against It

Dark Persuasion is the act of changing someone's mind, using techniques that are commonly used to affect someone's thinking, without them being aware of the persuasion. Some of the major tools for Dark Persuasion are Brainwashing, Hypnosis, Manipulation, and Deception. Below, these concepts will be discussed more in-depth.

Brainwashing

Brainwashing is unique because it has a codified method. If you look closely, you will see the steps of brainwashing used in many different domains of life and by many different organizations. They are used by cults, governmental operations, businesses, advertising, news media, and in many other ways. Brainwashing comes down to specific steps. First, a person is broken down from their sense of self. A healthy, typical person has a certain sense of self, which gives them their identity and confidence. A person's sense of self is what allows them to function in the world without becoming subject to undue persuasion or suggestibility. The first part of brainwashing is breaking this down to make the person more suggestible.

This takes many forms; it could be that the person is told that they are not valid and worthy of respect. It could be that the person is put through physical challenges and not left alone to be able to relax or take their time doing anything. It could be verbal or physical. The breaking down of the self basically serves to make the person more likely to latch onto the ideas that the brainwasher wants them to believe. By breaking down the person's sense of self, they no longer believe in themselves, but rather believe in the person who is doing the brainwashing. This is something that is most prominently seen in the military.

The breaking down of self can be described as an assault on the identity of the person. A person with an identity knows who they are. A person without an identity can be formed into whoever you want them to be. Guilt is a big part of this process. Sometimes, people are told that they have done something very wrong in their past. This is often seen with cults. Cults will tell a person that they are bad and essentially guilty and shameful as a person. This serves to get the people to think badly about themselves and look towards the outside for happiness instead of the inside.

This external motivation for acceptance and forgiveness is often an essential part of the brainwashing process. For typical healthy people, they have a sense within themselves that tells them that they are good and have a place in the world. This can be known as self-concept. Of course, everyone needs some external validation, and we all need relationships in which we feel loved and accepted. However, when a person depends on external validation for all of their needs of self-worth, they become very susceptive to toxic relationships and brainwashing.

The person who is being brainwashed is given the opportunity to "confess" for their new community. This makes them think that they can only share their lives with the brainwashed, and they start to think that this is the only way they can be happy. The group or individual who is doing the brainwashing will tell them that they have leniency and that they are capable of forgiving the person. In reality, there is no need to forgive the person, because they have done nothing wrong. The brainwasher is creating a false sense of dependency and they are creating the dynamic that makes the person feel like they depend on this person for their salvation.

The person gives their confession, and they channel their guilt into this dynamic. Their guilt has been built up so much that they feel the need to release it somehow, and the brainwasher lets them release their guilt into the group, and they are "forgiven". After this process happens, the person is psychologically tied to their brainwashers, and they start to think subconsciously that this is their new home, their new family.

After this process has been completed once or more than once, the person who is being brainwashed is subjected to another process. This time, the person is told that they are the best that they are brilliant and good and they are loved and accepted. This is part of the "rebuilding" phase. In this phase, the person is built back up, but in the context of the group/cult mindset. So, instead of them building healthy self-esteem on their own, they are only building self-esteem to fit into the new brainwashed context. This makes it so that the person cannot see themselves outside of this contest. They think that if they leave the cult, they will not be accepted by mainstream society, because they were accepted by the cult first and only.

This is the basic structure of brainwashing. This process may be repeated time and time again to ensure that the person is firmly ensnared into the group dynamic.

Hypnosis

Hypnosis is the next major application of Dark Persuasion that will be discussed. Hypnosis can occur with or without the person's knowledge. If a person knows they are being hypnotized, they may be more aware of what is going on, but they are still susceptive to manipulation.

Hypnosis is used for many different reasons, and it can be used for positive change as well as negative change. Hypnosis has several elements, and they may or may not be present in different iterations of the hypnosis process. It starts with an induction. Remember in cartoons, when they have the illustration of the swirling visual effect, and some head-wrapped mystic is holding a watch with the swirl in front of a person's face? This cartoon depiction is what is known formally as the induction process.

The induction process is when a person is actually trying to change another person's state of consciousness. In order to make the person more suggestible and influence-able, hypnosis uses an actual transformation of the state of consciousness. In order to think about this, you can think about a person who is typical and awake, a person who is paralyzed but otherwise capable, and a person who is in a coma. There are many graduations to the state of consciousness that a person is in. The person who is being hypnotized is not paralyzed, but they are closer to that than normal consciousness. Normal consciousness allows the person to have too much stability and defenses. The state that is induced in hypnosis is one where a person does not have all their defenses in play.

After the induction process has been successfully implemented, then the person can be told what to do or what to think. Since the person who is being hypnotized has their defenses uncovered and weakened, they are able to take instructions without question.

One method that works in NLP as a tool for hypnosis is anchoring. Anchoring is when a hypnotist uses something very familiar to you to bring you to that induction space where you are very suggestible. It might be a nursery rhyme, it might be a name you were called when you were younger, or it might be a song. This works to engage your subconscious and it tricks you into thinking you are safe and allowed to be engaged in the suggestions.

Another NLP –based method for hypnosis is the NLP Flash. The flash works by switching the reward to punishment, or the punishment to a reward. So, if there is something that you like to do which you are trying to stop doing, like smoking cigarettes, the hypnotist will make you think about a cigarette, and then they will make you experience something very uncomfortable, like an electric shock or some other kind of physical or emotional pain. This is a very dark method and can have very deep implications.

Hypnotism can be a very strong way to persuade someone against their will. It may not be as secretive as the other methods of persuasion, but it can be used without your knowledge.

The next major method of Dark Persuasion is manipulation. Manipulation comes in many forms; what we will talk about most here is manipulation in interpersonal relationships. Manipulators have many methods, but some of the major ones will be discussed in the following paragraphs.

The first is putting down the other person. The manipulator often will have to be very sneaky about this technique. Obviously, if there is someone who puts you down, you will not like them and you will start to avoid them. So, the manipulator often starts out as a close friend or a confidant. They build trust in the relationship before diving in. Then, at some point, they will start to disparage the other person in what they do, how they look, or other parts of their personality. The manipulator often knows exactly how much they can push buttons and they know how far they can go before being recognized as a manipulator. Along with their technique also comes the guilting of the other person. The manipulator makes the other person feel like they have wronged them, rather than the truth, which is that they are being tricked. They manipulator will make the person feel like they have some sort of debt to the other so that they enter into a sort of pact where there is inequality. Ultimately, what happens is that the manipulator puts the person down, which makes them feel bad about themselves, and it makes them feel like they don't deserve to stand up for themselves.

Another technique of manipulation is lying. Lying may be one of the more straightforward techniques of the manipulator. They will use excuses and complete fabrications to get other people to behave the way they want to. Lying is something that can start small and morph into a larger problem. The manipulator knows how to keep a person stuck in their web of illusions. Overall, they create a larger illusion of what the "truth" is. They try to create something that appears true to the manipulated person. The lies might have to do with any number of subjects. If the manipulator wants money, they might lie about how poor they are, and make themselves seem broke and desperate. If they want loyalty, they might make up lies about how important the other person is to them. If they want a job, they might lie about their experience in that field and make it sound like they are very successful. If they want sex, they might lie about a whole host of subjects.

Deception

Deception is the last major method of Dark Persuasion that we'll talk about. Deception is similar to lying, but it has some different components. One of them is equivocation. Equivocation is when someone makes vague or ambiguous statements. The point is to make things unclear so that you are not able to point out the mistake in their logic. Deception is making things seem a certain way when they are not that way. Deception is when a person uses any tactics to help make a situation seem different than it is. Lying by omission is one example of this. Lying by omission is when a person leaves out important information for the sake of changing others' perception of reality. Deception is done without a person's knowledge and it is something that changes their perception of the situation without actually lying. Camouflage is another example of this deception technique. This happens when someone is trying to hide the truth in a way that another person won't realize that they are missing some of the necessary parts of the story. This will be used when someone is employing half-truths. Camouflage will happen when somebody is trying to hide their real name or what they do for work. Camouflaging can be conceptualized as a way to hide in plain sight, in metaphoric terms. A person who is skilled in employing camouflage will be able to change their entire persona, including body language, when necessary.

One unique, more specific strategy, which is often used in Dark Persuasion, is the "give and take". The give and take technique works by fitting you into a dialogue about whatever the subject matter at hand is. The "give and take" technique works because a tricks people into thinking that they are actually in an equal relationship when they are not. People tend to trust those who they engage in a back-and-forth with. They start to think that, because there is a feedback loop, they are in a relationship that is fair. This is often not the case. One way to do this is to ask for someone to do a small favor for you. Once they have done the small favor, you then require that they do something else for you. Once both of these are completed, you pay them back. This might be by doing a small favor for them. It might be by offering some kind of material response, like money. Money is one of the biggest motivators for humans living in our time. Now, by establishing this loop of the give and take, you have established a relationship.

Emotional Intelligence and Assertiveness

Emotional intelligence is really about is to be yourself and handle others in the world that you live in. In order to do this, you must think about assertiveness and how much you need to assert yourself in your life. This will be a balance, as some people will need to find out that they might assert themselves a little too much in some relationship nod that they need to back off. Others will find that they don't assert themselves enough and that they need to be more assertive in life.

People who are easily manipulated are often not very assertive people. They tend to lack the confidence to question others and say what they mean. Being assertive means saying clearly and kindly and confidently what you really mean. The saying goes: say what you mean, mean what you say, doesn't see it mean. This means that you should say whatever is on your mind. You should find a way to be acceptable reasonably nice to whoever is in our company, and most of the time, you should be able to find a way to say something with generosity and respect to whoever is in the room. However, say what you mean, and whatever that is, that is your truth.

You must learn to speak your truth. Don't speak someone else's truth, they will not be able to channel yours. Don't expect other people to speak for you. Only you know your truth, and you have the power to share it with the world or to tuck it away.

The hawk knows that it flies, at night or during the day, and it knows where it goes knows where it has been. The hawk knows a noble purpose and it does its best to be the best hawk that it can be. The beautiful thing about animals is that they are always trying to the best that they can be because there is no alternative in the animal kingdom.

Assertiveness means that when you have a question, you ask it. Don't let people just assume what you think, what you feel, what you want. Tell them what you feel. You are the controller of your own destiny, and you determine your own success.

Knowing yourself is an Art

Being able to protect yourself from manipulation involves keeping knowledge of how we see the world and how we move in the world in order to be able to observe others. This is why knowing yourself is so important. It takes a lot of intuition to understand how other people see you in the world, and this can cue you into their behavior.

One way to start this is to look at the system of personality, like the Enneagram or astrology, and see what lines up most with you. This can tell you about what drives you have in your personality that you might not even realize. When you are trying to find out what type of personality you are, you are engaging in a self-reflexive behavior that will help you to be a better person. If it will help you to know you and your intuition will be increased as a part of this.

Another way to know oneself is to participate in the art or to watch or listen to the art. A movie can tell us the story of a world. It is a way by which we understand the world. Each time that you talk, you are telling a story, whether it is in words, or in the way that you speak the words. This can help to see yourself of the weaknesses and strengths that you have.

When you are reading a great novel, you become immersed in that book, and you get to share a little bit of the writers' world in your imagination. The writer and reader create a continuum, wherein the writer's consciousness is being followed directly by another person. They say that literature is the art that most people can actually escape their world and get into another person's consciousness.

You start to learn the characters, and you start to predict what they are about to do. Characters in the story can be compared to people you know in real life, and the book can give your ideas about your own behavior and change the world in your actions. As you go out through the story, you are experiencing a ride that is the most joyous way of expressing ourselves. This is art.

Art is a mysterious way that we participate in the world. Art has the power to incite wars and peace. It is a way that you can deeply disturb people and you can keep them happy and calm. Art (we are talking here about the art with a big A, as to mean every category of art, from dance to film to sculpture) is a way that we are in the world that lets us start a feedback loop with the world, and it becomes a source of communication with the world and with others. This is a way that we can find solace and express ourselves to the world.

Art is also a way that we immortalize ourselves. Each human is subject to the lifespan that they are given on this planet, and when you realize that your life is going to end eventually, you start to realize that the world will move on without you. This means that you might be forgotten, at least according to our primal fear. So, we try to do things to counteract this. The most primal and animal way is to have children because then you'll live on in the world through the people who you have created to carry out their own goals and happiness in the world.

Art is a way that you can do an analysis on yourself to deeper levels. Remember the Rorschach test, a way of analyzing people where we look at blobs of ink of paper and say whatever comes to mind first? Well, all art is sort of like that, as a creator and as a viewer. As a creator, when you are creating the art, you are creating the ink blob. Sometimes it is very clear what the artist is talking about. When you look at a Norman Rockwell painting, you understand the scene that he has created because he is putting you right there in a scenario that you can recognize and understand. Other times, the artist is putting you in a place where you can't understand because you aren't meant to. This kind of art can help us to explore what it feels like to other people to experience part of that world. Abstract art is not about telling you things but rather gets you to think.

Many people say that literature is the way that you can most experience another persons' consciousness, out of all of the art forms. Think about the best book you ever read. You were so into it that you couldn't put it down, and when you read it, you were nowhere else except in the world created by the writer. You were a citizen in his world, and there was nothing to do except to be there in the story and experience whatever was going on.

When you do this, you are experiencing a human mode called flow. Flow is when you are just in the moment, when you are only experiencing something that you are doing, like meditating, playing piano, running, driving, or something else. It is a state of focus and a state of creativity.

In order to know yourself, you have to be able to experience the extremes of life. You must have been able to understand the anger and express it. You must know when you feel angry and know what that feels like to you. You must be able to experience joy at the highest level, for this is an extremely human feat. You must be able to take deep pain and failure and also accept the beauty in life. You must be able to immerse yourself in the book and then go pay some bills that you have lying around, which is just menial work that you have to do. There are all sorts of things that you have to deal with that are big and small, and none is less important. It might seem that the small stuff is less important, and in many ways, it is, but the details are something that you can be vigilant with, and they are ways for you to let yourself really experience each part of life.

The number-one way to do this concretely every day and learn about you is journaling. You can journal every day a never write the same thing twice. Journaling doesn't have to be your homework. It can be fun, it can be creative and it can be a way to release yourself from the shackles of what binds you.

When you write about yourself, you are looking at yourself through the lens of another person, or at least not through your own. By writing about yourself, you are also able to tell your story. Let's talk about both of these aspects of writing.

When you write about yourself, you get to look at yourself through your own eyes, but in a more objective way. Or at least, that's the hope. When you open up the journal and start writing about yourself, and it is all negative stuff, then you should be able to tell yourself that you have a problem there. When you are writing about yourself, try to be as subjective as possible. When you find that you are not able to do this, it might mean that you are too much up in your head.

You see, we start to develop ideas and concepts about ourselves that may or may not be true. Even if they are true, they might not be so good to dwell on. Many people have problems with invasive thoughts or automatic negative thoughts. If you are one of these people, just take your writing and see if you notice these thoughts in writing, and see if you can stop yourself and try to write out thoughts that are kinder and more accurate.

By talking about writing about ourselves in a more objective way, we can get more in touch with ourselves in terms of our real desires, goals, and ways of living. When we are in our heads, we don't get a really good idea of our perceptions vs. the world's perceptions around us. When we are all up in our heads about how we are, the world seems like a movie that we are starring in. When we write about our lives, you are writing a movie. An objective perspective will let you talk about yourself as a friend rather than yourself. You can start to think of this guy or girl as a person who is closer to the world than to your own experience, and when you do that you reduce the number of feelings and thoughts that might get mixed up with the perspective. When you take out the emotions and thoughts and just go with the facts, you'll find that you can be fairer and more realistic about yourself. Some people will find that they have self-esteem issues that they need to deal with. Others will be more on the side of narcissism and they will need to learn about how to reduce their selfishness and start to think more about others.

Everyday Persuasion Techniques

The first persuasion technique that will be discussed is reframing. Reframing is a concept that is often used to help people be more positive in their lives. Rather than saying, "the glass is half empty", you can say, "the glass is half full", and this will create the feeling that you are actually doing better than you think. Either way, the glass is filled with the same amount of liquid. It is just the way that you frame the situation that will manipulate people. Sometimes, you may want to make things seem direr than they are. In that case, it might be more useful to say that the glass is actually emptier than it is full. Politicians are extremely good at this technique, and they will often use it to score political points. The news media also uses this technique to bolster certain candidates or ideas. When something bad has happened to a candidate that they support, they will bring up all the good things about the situation. They will find some way that the bad thing is actually good for the world or for other people.

The trick here is to use language that will make something evoke certain emotions in a person. If a person is trying to make something sound worse than it is, they will often try and bring up words that have negative emotional connotations.

Another technique is mirroring. Mirroring what a person does or says can create the illusion that you have more empathy for them. It makes them identify with you and it makes it seem like you're on the same page. A person who is very skilled at this will be able to morph into a different personality around different people. Actors should be especially good at this. Mirroring is a great way to make people think that you are on their side.

False scarcity is another thing that people use to make things seem dire. False scarcity is when something is made out to be rare. People might say, "oh, a good English teacher? That's really rare in this day and age." This is just one example. Whatever the subject is, it is probably not true that there are no other options. By making it seem like there are no other options, you are starting to create the environment for the other person to say yes to whatever you want them to. False scarcity feeds into people's fear and self-preservation instincts. After all, nobody wants to be left alone or without resources.

Reciprocation can be used to create an obligation. This is a trick that is used by people in tourist areas who are looking to make a few bucks. These people will do something like shine your shoes or clean your windshield, without asking you, and then will ask for money in return for the service. This is an effective technique that often works well. This is done without your request. Even if you have not asked them to shine your shoes or clean your windshield, they do it anyway. Now that they have done something for you, you feel obligated to give them something in return.

Another technique involves using timing to your advantage. When people are tired, they are more likely to be open or vulnerable to manipulation. When people are in the hot sun, they are likely to pay more for a cold drink. It is all about the context. When people are at the movie theater, they want to partake in movie snacks like popcorn or candy. Since the movie theater is the only place that is selling these things, they will pay much more than if they were somewhere else. It is all about creating value that is based on the moment. This can be particularly helpful if you are trying to incorporate persuasion into your business plans. Have you ever encountered a very efficient salesperson? It is likely that they shook your hand at some point in the encounter. This seems like a very small move without repercussions, but the cognitive subconscious results are actually profound. A handshake represents a closed deal. By giving you the handshake before you have actually made any kind of deal, you are already starting to associate making a deal with this person. It is a small way to persuade, but it is effective.

Which leads us to our next technique, which is physical touch. Physical touch is a very powerful thing, and it can lead to a connection that is more visceral and subconscious than conscious. Physical touch makes you think that you are close to this person. It creates a physical feedback loop that the other person will want to continue in some other way than physical touch.

And, lastly, one of the most major and effective techniques for persuasion is confidence. If you are able to speak confidently and carry yourself with the air of confidence that you need to convince someone, you will be able to persuade him or her that you are someone to follow. Try to reduce your "like" and "Um" in your speaking. These make you seem humble and unsure. Speaking and acting confidently can help you to appear more confident than you are.

Differentiation

Differentiation is a process that happens when we are young children. There is a lot of research out there about parenting and the early years of childhood development. This is a time when the child must establish a permanent, trusting, deep bond with the mother, and father, and then at a certain point, start to understand themselves as a different person than their parents. At the very beginning, as is the mystery of life, we are fused with another person – literally part of another person. As we enter the world, we begin to exist independently in our own body. But that link is still there. After a while, a person learns to develop intimate relationships and also be very independent. This is what a generally well-functioning person is able to do: have very close moments of intimacy, long-term relationship with intimacy, and also be confident in oneself, able to take care of oneself, and to be able to tolerate long periods of independence.

Some people have issues with this than others. Parents may notice that their child's attachment is insecure or avoidant; they might recognize their child pulling g away at certain times or never wanting to be without the parent. These can be signs that the child has not developed a sufficiently mature level of differentiation.

As another example of differentiation, let us take high school as an example. High school kids tend to love fads and to go with the latest "cool" thing, whether it is a movie, music, type of shoes, or whatever else. Let's say that at a certain high school, there is a new Superman movie out. It gets out that this is the coolest movie experience of the year, and everyone "must" see it. Their peers are influencing them, and many will end up watching the movie, whether or not it is a good movie. There tends to be safety in numbers, and people inherently understand that. So when George, a 10th grader who has exceptional taste in film, says at the lunch table that he respectfully did not enjoy the new Superman movie, and is able to express his opinion calmly and with an open mind, he is demonstrating a high level of differentiation for his age.

Another thing that comes along with differentiation is honesty. It takes confidence to be honest. If you are always worried about what other people are going to think about our personal preferences and habits, you will find yourself very alienated.

The opposite of differentiation is co-dependency. This is a behavior and relationship pattern. Sometimes it is passed down through generations. It is a condition that affects your ability to have a healthy and mutually satisfying relationship. It can be known as a sort of relationship addiction. People who are co-dependent usually end up in relationships that are one-sided. These relationships may be destructive or abusive. This kind of relationship can be common in families affected by alcoholism or addiction. Co-dependency can affect spouses, parents, siblings, friends, or co-workers. The phrase originally comes from describing the dynamics in families with addictions. You can also see this pattern, however, in families that have not experienced this. It becomes a way of being in the world.

A healthy level of differentiation is necessary in order to keep yourself from falling prey to dark manipulation. The people who have not developed this are the people who get involved in cults and schemes in which they are taken advantage of.

Chapter 4: Unmask the Dark Persuader

The tactics of Dark Persuasion and Dark Psychology are used around us every day. From car dealerships to governmental organizations, to interpersonal relationships, dark persuasion tactics are something you always have to look out for. So how do you protect yourself from being persuaded against your will? It takes some self-knowledge and exploration, but you'll be able to unmask the dark persuader if you give it some thought. Awareness is a huge part of the journey.

First, you should try to learn about your responses in certain situations. The car dealership is a great example of this. When you go into a sales situation, you should recount your goals before entering and try to center yourself. Then, as you enter into the battle of the sales situation, you should try to recognize your responses to the situation as challenges come up.

The dealer might try to tell you what you want. This is a common method of dark persuasion for people who are trying to sell you something. The salesperson will tell you, sometimes quite literally, that you want something that they have, even if it is something that you don't need or want. When someone tells you this, what is your response? Are you able to tell them no, I don't want that? How are you able to get away from their advances?

It takes some strength of personality to pull this off, after all, persuasive people can be very difficult to go against the grain with. When the dealer tells you that they have a car that you have to have, and they start to pressure you, try to see how you feel in your body at that moment. Are you feeling grounded? If not, try and remember that you have two feet on the floor and you are there in space, standing somewhere. You are not floating above the ground. You are strong and planted in your position.

Another way to maintain grounded ness is to relax. Don't let someone get all up in your face and make you feel uncomfortable.

You should remember that whatever you are doing is your right and your place to be doing. You have earned it, and you have the power. When you allow your body to get uncomfortable and for stress to manifest in your body, you allow yourself to become ungrounded and uncentered, and this will lead you a lack of strength. People who are weak are more easily persuaded.

People who are grounded, strong, and centered are not easily persuaded of things, which they don't believe in. People who are weak are more easily persuaded. Why is this? You can think of human relationships and cognition somewhat like a gravitational pull. A planet, or any large mass in outer space, has a certain gravitational pull, which will pull in objects with a mass in outer space into its orbit. They will then be locked into orbit with the planet, and they will be connected, in a sense, to the planet. This is similar to human spirits. We are all sort of floating around, so to speak, and we get sucked into the gravitational pull of other planets and large masses. Their power and persuasiveness serve as the pull of gravity, and before you know it, we are stuck and connected to them.

This happens a lot with people who lose their family or support system. Left without people to help you out, you are easily susceptible to tricks of the mind and persuasive techniques. You should make sure that you have a positive support system to help you out if you feel that you are going up against someone who is using dark manipulation tactics.

Another important aspect of preventing yourself from being persuaded is confidence. If you have confidence in yourself that you will be able to face against someone who is trying to persuade you and come away wholly yourself, safe, and accomplishing your goals, you will be more likely to be able to do it than someone who is not confident. Confidences are something that goes against all the principles of dark persuasion. Someone using dark persuasion principles is not counting on meeting someone who is confident in their web of deceit. They are looking for the people who have no sense of self, the people who have nothing to say when you ask, "who are you?"

Intuition

Intuition is key here. Sometimes, it may be difficult to tell who is using dark persuasion techniques, whether it is for their goals or some other overarching goal of an organization, or whatever. Intuition is key to being able to detect when these techniques are being used against you. Let's say you start a new job. It is a sales job, and you are taken to a group interview where you are asked to convince the manager that you are good for the job. Group interviews, well, they aren't the best sign, but you are looking for a job right now and need the money, and you decide, whatever, you will go have a look. You do well in the group interview and you are selected as one of the people who will be joining the team. You start the training process and you notice that something is off. When you are participating in the training, you are shown videos and told how to operate in the company. You start to notice that some of the videos tend to denigrate the people who are being trained. You notice that people go along with it, and agree that this job is very honorable and that they should be ashamed of their past. The management then goes on to try and convince you that this job is one of the only jobs that are out there and that this is the only job you'll be able to get, so you better not quit. Then, you are started to be told how wonderful the benefits are, and that you might be able to make a fortune at this job if you work hard.

You should pay attention to your intuition in this situation because it should be warning you about every single one of these persuasion tactics.

Your intuition will be able to recognize these as malevolent because we have a natural sense of self-protection as humans. Evolutionarily, we have become accustomed to trying to protect ourselves in the wild. Before humans developed an agricultural system and modern civilization, people had to defend themselves from the pure elements of the world, which were very threatening. People had no sense of what might be happening in nature or with animals; there was no science to tell us about the weather, no books to read about the history of the world, no way to know whether it is going to snow tomorrow or rain the next day. An earthquake could be seen as a very terrifying and mystifying event.

Through the centuries of living like an animal in the wild, humans have developed an evolutionary capacity for understanding their intuition. Intuition is something that is very hard to understand. It is not exactly thinking or cognition, it is not a feeling, it is somewhere in between. It is a gut instinct that tells you when you are being played. It can also tell you when you are experiencing true love, and when you should jump into something with your whole heart. But intuition has a great capacity to protect us. Your intuition will be going off when someone is trying to use dark persuasion techniques against you. You just need to learn how to tune into intuition.

Learning to tune into intuition might be a difficult task, but you will get there eventually. Think about times in the past when you were able to detect someone lying. Maybe you saw a little smile in the corner of their mouth, or maybe the story just didn't add up. Whatever it was that allowed you to get some insight into their condition, that's what intuition is. Intuition is letting yourself trust yourself to see into someone else's soul. We all have that capacity, and in fact, we all have the capacity to read peoples' minds. It is just something that people rarely recognize and even less often learn to develop and embrace.

Another important part of defending yourself from dark persuasion tactics is to learn how to say no. Saying no, in all its different forms, is what will save you from being put into the grinder. Sometimes saying no is putting the answer off. This is called the delay tactic. By not giving an answer now, you are delaying the need to give an answer at all, and this gives you time to think about your options and consider whether or not you are being manipulated for some purposes that are not for your best interest. This is a great tactic in situations that involve sales or personal relationships. By saying, "give me some time to think about it", you are allowing yourself some time away from the pressure at the moment to really give some thought to the idea of if you are being true to yourself.

The delay method is a good tactic to defend yourself from dark persuasion because much of dark persuasion tactics rely on a person being pressured in the heat of the moment. If you are able to get out of that moment, and you are able to rely on deeper thinking and a better environment that will foster relaxation and calmness, you will inevitably make a better decision regarding the task at hand.

Machiavellianism as Defense Mechanism

Another thing to consider is using Machiavellian principles to defend yourself. You should ask yourself if whatever is being presented puts you further away from your personal goals or closer to your personal goals. This will allow you to evaluate who is the winner of each situation. Remember, you should be focused on yourself in this mindset. This is not the mindset of helping people, although there are obviously many situations in which it is better to not adopt a Machiavellian mindset. If you are in a situation where you need to provide support for other people, or if you are in a situation in which you already trust the person you are encountering, the Machiavellian mindset is not appropriate. However, when you are trying to defend yourself from manipulative people or people who do not have your best interests in mind, you can lean on this mindset to help put up defenses.

The Machiavellian mindset is, at its core, selfishness. Most people think of selfishness as a negative thing. However, you should rethink this. Selfishness is a very necessary human trait. It is not something that you should employ all the time, by any means, but you should be able to use selfishness when it appropriate. After all, in a situation where you are being challenged with dark persuasion, it is you against them. It is a fight or be killed. So, in order to defend yourself, you must become selfish. Your foe in this battle does not deserve help or kindness. You are the one who deserves help and kindness from yourself. Do not give them an inch. Ask yourself what is best for you at that moment, whether it lets the other person down or not. Some people are so wired against this, that it becomes a challenge for them. Some people are so wired towards being a helper and a giver that standing up for themselves is very foreign and it is very different for them. You might find that this is true for you, and you will have to switch over from a mindset of a helper and pushover into someone who is self-interested and wants to help themselves.

Understand the Motive

When you can detect that you are being manipulated or persuaded, the first step is to examine what the motivation is for the manipulator. What is it that you have that they want? This could be many things, and one of the most common is money. When you are presented with a situation where you are being persuaded to do something, you should first examine the possibility of monetary gain. If it is a business that is soliciting you for time or patronage, ask yourself if you need those services, and ask if your life is better off with or without those services. If it is a charitable organization, do some research into whether they do what they say and if they should be trusted?

There are also other reasons that people might be trying to sue you. In this day and age, data is very valuable. There are many ways that people are subjected to scams that get you to provide information about what you do online or other activities. This may seem fairly benign at first, but if you look into it, you will realize that you are being taken advantage of. The way that development companies for apps and other online services work these days is that they look for ways to collect information about you. Why is this information valuable? Because it helps them to be able to target other people in their services and manipulation.

Remember, if the situation is not equitable, you are probably being manipulated. In order to unmask the dark persuader, you should be able to see why entering into some kind of agreement actually benefits you rather than the agreement being one-sided.

Get to the Root of Things

Human psychology is such that we are pointed to ignore the deeper levels of our situations so that we can survive. The will to survive is very implicit and deep in the consciousness of a human. We have all kinds of automatic responses and habit patterns that become standard parts of our lives. We do not question them. They become ingrained in the everyday truth with which we live. So, in order to develop critical thinking and problem skills, we have to learn how to get to the root of things. This will take some introspection and you try to break down the repression and suppression of thoughts and feelings that have built up. This is not uncommon; many people have repressed ideas, thoughts, and desires, and never observe them or become aware of them. Getting to the root of the problem takes determination. It takes bravery to look inside the soul this is our takes, ultimately: to look inside the soul. If you can trust your instincts, you will be able to think critically and solve problems at the deepest level. If you put a band-aid on the wound, you will treat the symptom but not the cure. In order for us to understand the nuance that exists in most of our interpersonal and personal problems, we must be able to detach from emotion and look at ourselves with pure determination.

This requires us not to get distracted by petty or unreasonable desires. When we are faced with a problem, we must ask ourselves: are we really getting down to the underlying causes? Take for example the case of Ben, an eighth-grader at Higgins Middle School. Ben is a smart kid and has a great head on his shoulders. However, he has developed some behavioral problems. He seems to have gotten stuck in a scenario where his only friends are ones who cause trouble. They cause the distraction of other students, disruption in class, and vandalize parts of the school without getting caught. Ben is not a bad kid; he likes excitement and adventure, and these activities provide him with a sense of challenge and excitement. He takes on these rule-breaking activities and uses his sense of critical thinking to get away with it. His teachers try to tell Ben to stay away from these friends because they are a bad influence on him. They punish him for being distracting. Ben is given detention once a week for the next three months. What the teachers are thinking is that if they use behavioral modification to try and punish the boy for bad behavior he will learn the rules and want to avoid the behaviors. What they are ignoring, however, is that Ben has family troubles at home, and not experiencing the sense of stability he needs. This is getting to the root of the problem. The problem is not the symptom behaviors that come out as a result. The root of the problem is Ben's family life. He doesn't feel grounded in his family life and is not able to play the role of a successful student in school, as he would like. The root of the problem here is much more important than the symptoms. Ben should be recommended to the school counselor so that he can express his feelings in a safe space. If he is able to deal with the stressors that are involved in his family life, he will be able to focus more in school.

If you are easily manipulated, you will be easily convinced that Ben's problems are whatever his teacher says they are. Why? Because they want to take the easy way out. Teachers can often be very manipulative with parents because they want nothing less than to have to really investigate the problem. Partly because it is not their job, and partly because people tend to want to do the least amount of work possible?

Getting to the root of the problem will require you to do a lot of investigation. People will try to get in your way; you must detach from emotion and try to be a neutral observer. This is where using critical thinking skills is very important, you must cut through the silliness to get to the essence of a problem The essence of a problem could be something that is totally unexpected. You must remain open to the chance that the solution you are seeking is right under your nose, or right under something else that your eyes have already crossed. Getting to the root of the problem requires persistence. How good you are at looking people dead in the eyes and disagreeing with them this will be easier for some than others.

Persistence requires knowledge to back up your claims, and it requires confidence in your actions and confidence in yourself as a person. Persistence can come from many things. Some parents like to encourage their kids to get involved in sports for this reason. Athletic training can sometimes provide modeling and techniques to become a persistent, excelling person. So what happens if you run into Stacy in accounting and she doesn't agree with the deadline that is perfectly reasonable and that you have the right to set? You must get to the root of the problem first, take into account all of the information that is already available. This could be experienced in the past with Stacy, it could be files that you have that she has met deadlines on in the past, or it could be her emails that she had recently sent to you. Whatever data you have to gather, make sure you have compiled it and maintained an awareness of all of the information that you already have.

Chapter 5: Understanding the Subconscious Mind

Philosophers have long debated the different realms of the mind. Since ancient times, thinkers have discussed and written about the different parts of the psyche; there are the parts that are dedicated to loving, to thinking about material things, to artisticness, to combativeness. However, to talk about the subconscious, we must talk about Freud. Sigmund Freud was one of the most important psychologists and philosophers in the history of man. He lived around the turn of the 19th century, and it was he who developed the concept of psychoanalysis.

The Subconscious in Psychology

Psychoanalysis is a method of uncovering unconscious material through various methods of applied therapy. By sitting on a couch and talking about whatever arose in the person's mind, Freud would be able to analyze that person's life and unconscious motives. Freud believed that people are driven by deep, instinctual, sexually-centered drives. He believed that our animal nature was a considerable part of our psyche and that what we presented to the world was only a small part of the equation.

Think about an iceberg; there is a part that is visible above the water, and that is the conscious mind. What do we mean by the conscious mind? It is the part of the mind, which is thinking, feeling, and expressing itself at the moment. It is the conscious source of material that is easily accessible. The top of the iceberg is the smallest part of the iceberg, however, and if you dive deeper, you can see that most of the iceberg exists underwater. This is what Freud thought about the proportionality of the human psyche. He thought that most of the human psyche was not at the surface, but rather down below in the depths. Most of the unconscious was down where it was difficult to access, and he thought that people didn't really show their true selves unless they were put in a position where this material could be uncovered.

Freud called the different parts of the psyche the ego, the superego, and the id. The Id is the part of us, which is animal in nature. T is the part of us that wants to have sex, eat, and fight. It is the most primal part of humanity and it is the only part of the psyche, which is within us from the very moment that we are born. It might seem dark and scary, but it is the most natural part of us.

The Ego is the part of the psyche, which is grounded in reality. It is the part, which tells us what is doable and controls our reality orientation. The Ego is the part of us, which "converts" the Id's drives into behavior.

The Super Ego is the moral component of our psyche. The superego is what tells us what is appropriate and moral in any given circumstance and it tells us what we think is okay and what we think is unacceptable.

The Id and the Ego are being engaged when people use Dark Psychology and Dark Persuasion. When a person is using these tactics, they are engaging the subconscious, which partly lives in the id and partly lives in the ego.

The subconscious mind is made up of all the memories and associations that you have, and all the experiences with different people that you have. Have you ever tired a portion of food that you had a particularly bad reaction to, or gotten food poisoning? His happens to many people, and many of them discover that after this experience, they are no longer able to eat that food again, for many years. This is the subconscious at work. If the food in question is carrots, then you will find that the next time you encounter carrots, you will be disgusted at the thought of eating them. You will find them repulsive and unnatural. This is because your subconscious has internalized the experience of discomfort and disgust with that particular food. In reality, you know that the food will be fine in future experiences, but you are not actually able to encounter that food and engage with yourself rationally, because you have integrated that bad experience into your psyche. The subconscious is instinctual and has plenty of animalistic qualities to it.

The subconscious is responsible for the sexual drives, which we have. It is governed by the pleasure principle, which basically states that we are driven by pleasure and that pleasure is the ultimate motivator. This is why advertising works so well when it engages ideas of sexual motivation and other forms of pleasure. The old saying "sex sells" is ever prescient to this day. Think about the phenomenon of sexual attraction. You might understand consciously that you are married, and happily so, but you will still find yourself wanting to engage in sexual conduct with others, even though you have agreed with your partner to not do so. This is the very essence of the id. It is always present, lurking, and it is the most animalistic pressure. In fact, sexuality is often part of Dark Persuasion tactics. A leader is often very attractive in physicality. This is part of charisma and it is a very effective way to engage in someone's subconscious drives.

Sexuality and other base drives are an important part of dark Persuasion. Since the dawn of time, humans have been subject to manipulation due to sexual urges. Sex and drugs have always been a way to control and manipulate a population.

Memory

Memory is a tricky thing. If two people witness an event, they will both have different accounts of that event. One person might remember it as a situation in which they were victimized. Another person might think of it as an event that was fair to all parties involved. Memory can fade and come back within a lifetime. Think about the earliest memory that you have. Undoubtedly, it will be one of your childhood. Is it a pleasant memory, or an unpleasant one? Sometimes the unpleasant memories are what stick out the most.

The mind has several different types of memory. First of all, there are the classifications of long-term memory and short-term memory. As the names would suggest, long-term memory is when you keep something in your mind for a very long time. Short-term memory is where thoughts or experiences are stored while your brain decides to file them in your long-term memory or to let go of them. Explicit memory is a type of long-term memory that will require conscious thought to bring about. This is what you are using when you try to think of your earliest memory. Implicit memory is something that you don't have to try for. This is riding a bike (if you've already learned to do so). That is something that people say never goes away. It is something that you already know how to do, and you don't have to try to do it. It is also the type of memory you are using when you brush your teeth or walk around. Your muscles do not have to be directed to do these things, because you already know how to do them. Autobiographical memory is your memory of how your life has progressed. This is something that almost everyone has, and it allows you to build a life story.

Subconscious memory is what you are using when you have a "bad feeling" about something. This is similar to intuition. These are very closely related concepts. Intuition and subconscious memory are when you are integrating memories of the past, but you don't know when or where they are coming from, and you don't exactly know the content of this memory. Many people use this type of memory when they are in situations that are dangerous.

This will be something you can lean on to identify instances when you are being manipulated or persuaded, brainwashed or deceived. FI you can tap into this mysterious system of the subconscious, you will be able to defend yourself. This is no easy task, and it takes a lot of trial and error and it takes experience.

Ten Ways to Train the Subconscious

1. Allow yourself to believe the unbelievable.

In order to change your habits or way of thinking, you must fight back against the impulse to believe that nothing can ever change. This is one thing that often gets people stuck; it is the belief that the way they are now will be the way they are forever. Banish this thought, for it will only leave you undeveloped and will keep you away from self-realization.

2. Give yourself permission to be successful.

Many people have in their subconscious the belief that they can never be as successful as they want. Some people have complexes from growing up poor that tell them that they will never have enough money and that they should always act as though having enough money will never be an option for them. We keep ourselves unsuccessful, as well in other ways. Some people think that they can't be creative, or they can't do a certain type of job. You just have to switch this thinking, and when you find these thoughts arising from your subconscious, you can tell yourself consciously that you are capable; you are able to be successful.

3. Resist others' projections.

We are all subject to the projection of others. Projection is when a person has beliefs or feelings about themselves, and they think that all other people are like them. They start to think that everyone around them is actually matching them in some sort of characteristic or habit. People will put you in a box, and expect you to act a certain way. You must allow yourself to totally reject their thoughts about you. Resist their attempts to put you in a box.

4. Give yourself some positive reinforcement.

The very essence of resisting Dark Persuasion is being able to understand the dark forces at work and giving yourself the opposite information. Being able to understand Dark Psychology means that you will have to engage in the darkness just a little bit. However, once you do this, you will have to balance out your energy with some positive thinking as well. If you are able to give yourself positive messages to balance out the negative darkness, you will find that you are able to overcome all manipulation and deception.

5. Be real about your success.

Don't be humble. Of course, being humble is a virtue, but only up to a point. Being humble will eventually lead to your downfall. You need to stand with Machiavelli on this point, and let yourself be able to praise yourself wholeheartedly. Individualism is one of the main tenets of Western culture, and this means embracing yourself, your needs, and your way of living. Celebrate yourself. Tell yourself that you are the one who deserves success. Be real about what you have already accomplished – chances are, you have accomplished a lot.

6. Envision your future.

Be bold about your future. If you are always envisioning a future that is full of pain and suffering, you will probably be working toward making that real. If you are able to create a future vision for yourself that is one of success and domination, you will be much closer to creating that in reality.

7. Point out your own weaknesses so that you can work on them.

Your subconscious will play tricks on you. Sometimes, it will make you think that you are perfect and have no flaws, when in fact, this is not the case. Most people have one or two areas that they can work on. If you are able to point these out to yourself, you will find that you are able to morph more closely towards self-realization.

8. Embrace gratitude.

Embracing gratitude is all about fostering a healthy self-image, which will help you on your path to self-realization. Some people have damaged their subconscious, and they get bitter and weakened because of past failures. You must learn to resist this urge, and you must find gratitude in the world. This will make your defenses stronger and it will teach you that there are things that are worthy of your pursuit of happiness.

9. Identify what you want, and get it.

Stop messing around and keeping yourself from getting what you want. If you don't know how to get it, then try to learn how to get it. If your goal is a certain career path, then ask someone if you can be his or her apprentice. If it is something you can learn on your own, do your research and start to learn how you can achieve this goal on your own. Read books, the internet, and ask other people about how they have achieved what you want to achieve.

10. Get rid of your attachment to the "how".

The "how" is not important. The "how" is what keeps you from getting what you want and need. This is where judgment comes in. The subconscious will sometimes push you towards judgment, and you will find that if you have a voice that pushes you towards judgment, this will start to create a space between what you want and where you are. You should work to reduce this space as much as possible.

Chapter 6: Charisma and Machiavellian Confidence

Confidence and charisma are ways to both employ dark psychological tactics on others as well as protect yourself from being manipulated by others. What do you think of when you think about confidence?

Rather than focusing on the modern conception of positive psychology's confidence, let's roll back the tape of history a little bit and consider Machiavelli's style of confidence. Machiavellianism is defined as a cold and calculating ability to work for and towards your own goals, for yourself. It does not emphasize morality or empathy, and it is an essentially cynical mindset.

Why cynical? The reason that this approach can be so successful boils down to the animal nature of human beings. Essentially, we are animals who are all trying to protect ourselves. Why? There are a few reasons. Some of us are focused on being able to extend the family line through the creation of the family. There is certainly a biological drive, and some would say a spiritual drive, to do so. Others are merely focused on the legacy of their own life, which is a worthy drive in and of itself.

Nice guys finish last. That's the mindset of Machiavellianism. It is all about strength. Cynicism helps to frame the world in a realistic way. People are out to get you and they want to stop you from accomplishing your goals. Think about it. There are not very many people who are actually just in the world. Justice is a concept that is very fluid, and it rarely is placed on the right people. The world is filled with predators, people who want to take advantage of other people. The world is filled with con artists, scams, businesses, mind control, brainwashing, and darkness.

That is not to say that there is no light in the world as well, but that's not what you have to worry about. You have to worry about being taken advantage of, you have to worry about protecting you and your family from evil. What kinds of evil? There are many kinds of pervasive evil in the world. Some of the kinds are ones that are already listed in this book. There are aloes other kinds, which have not been mentioned.

Machiavellian confidence is all about looking that evil in the face, realizing that it is there for a reason, and refusing to be taken advantage of. It is all about being stronger than the enemy.

First of all, you have to actually be stronger than the enemy, whatever that looks like for you. Physical strength is not everything, but some people feel much better if they put themselves in a place where they can be stronger than most other people. This will give you the upper hand in physical altercations, and it will also set you on a plane of development that will help in your pursuit of confidence. Confidence does not have to come from physical strength, however.

Some of the greatest kings who ever existed were small, wiry, and full of weakness in their physical body. What did they know how to do? They knew how to exercise their power of will. They knew how to motivate people, to get people behind them in their search for power, they knew how to drum up support and get people angry. Physical power can only take you so far. Then, you have to start thinking metaphysically.

Looking Inward

One thing that many people have to face to reach this state of confidence is to address their unfinished business. This is not business in the conventional meaning of the word. This is business in any form, whether it comes from past relationships, things that happened, things that you have been putting off for a while, or many other things. There can be many sources for unfinished business that have to be addressed.

Some people have relationships within their family that have to be addressed. We all didn't just one day appear as adults, we had to go through the process of development that every other human did. That means having a childhood. For many people, this must be addressed in order to reach the heights of confidence that we are talking about. Childhood contains many things: memories, reasons for living, habits formed, and personality created. Many people must look back on their childhood to make sense of what happened in order to find this place of Machiavellian confidence. Perhaps you were made to think that you have to always follow the rules when you were a child. This is how many people raise their children They raise them to think that you always have to fear and respect your elders, that you must bend your will to authority, and that you are not worthy of being an authority yourself. If this was how you were raised, you will have to address those experiences and push back against them. You must able to tell yourself that you are worthy of being an authority yourself, that you have the skill, power, and worth to be an authority in this world. You must tell that little child version of yourself that it's okay, you were told wrong, and now you are going to be powerful. On the other hand, if you were spoiled as a child, and told that you are already powerful and that you already have a fear of authority, even when you had not earned it, this will be something that you will have to learn as well. Confidence doesn't come from an unfounded place. You must learn to be humbled once or twice to actually earn what is called Machiavellian confidence. You can't learn this without failing a few times. Failure is what will show you your limits. When you are shown your limits, then you must go back and redefine them.

Unfinished business might be a romantic situation in which you felt that you were left in the lurch. Go back, do some writing and personal investigation, and see what you can find in that situation to make yourself integrate the experiences. Life is all about putting together the pieces of the puzzle that is your past. Once you put together the pieces of the puzzle, you'll be able to be yourself to higher consciousness.

Unfinished business can be based in habits that you already have. One of the most common is addiction. Addiction can be too many things. Sometimes it is drugs, sometimes it is alcohol, sometimes it is just thinking.

Many people develop an addiction to drugs in order to fill some void that they have in their thinking or other parts of their life. Drugs are often a way to make up for a loss of confidence or a lack of other strength characteristics.

An addict has two elements: dependence and denial. The dependence comes from some lack that exists in their lives. The denial is the lack of strength to know what you are addicted to something. The dependence usually comes from a place of missing something. This could be love, it could be confidence, and it could be a closeness with others. The lack usually has something to do with childhood, and it is something that people often don't understand until they are able to process their lives later on. The addict gets into the habit of learning that they can cope with the world in this particular way.

For example, if there is a young man who grows up and goes to college and starts drinking right away in college that is probably because he does not have the people skills or confidence to interact with others. When he was younger, he did not learn what it is like to be able to interact with other people and make friends without drinking. So, when he gets to college, he feels lost. He doesn't feel like h knows how to be himself when he is around other people he might feel that he is weird or uninteresting to the people. Whatever it is, it means that he doesn't fit in. It means that he feels that there is not a place for him. The effects of alcohol will ease this. Alcohol gives him a purpose. It greases the gears of social interaction and it lets him feel like he is able to be himself, to be loud, be confident, and express himself with whatever he wants to say.

You can see how there is a void here that has been filled with the drug experience. No matter how much you try and fill the void with that drug, it won't be fulfilled until you go back and figure out why you are missing something. That is what is known as unfinished business.

Unfinished business will keep you from being yourself. It will keep you from achieving the levels of confidence that are possible for all people. You must go back, learn, and work to achieve understanding for your past condition in order to be able to achieve the type of Machiavellian confidence that we are talking about.

Self-Realization

Self-realization is a term that comes from the humanistic school of psychology. It is a term that references the idea that each person has an authentic self inside somewhere that can be reached through the process of understanding the self and doing work to achieve a more authentic and real you.

Humanistic psychology posits that when we are born, we start to absorb whatever is around us like a sponge. We start to learn behaviors. At first, we are an essence. We are just ourselves. It is a heady concept to think about: that when you are born, you are purely yourself, nothing else, and as you go on, you start to learn personality traits and learned behaviors. As this progresses, you get further and further away from yourself. This is not necessarily true; there could be a parental system that helps very young people to be very authentic in their entire lives. However, most of us were raised by imperfect parents, and at a certain point, we learned how to cope with the world in ways that took us away from our natural selves. This is a hypothesis that is not necessarily true across the board, but it is a useful way of thinking to be able to understand the construct of the authentic self and self-realization. Self-realization is also influenced by Maslow's pyramid of needs.

The pyramid of needs is a system that describes what is the most necessary and needed parts of life. It stars with food, shelter, and the very basic necessities of life. Then, it moves into more extraneous parts of life, like work and fulfillment. At the top of the triangle is self-realization. How does this relate to Dark Persuasion and Machiavellian confidence?

In order to make it to the top of the pyramid in your life development, you will need to meet all of the previous requirements. This means learning what it is for you to have dependable, meaningful work, a love life, relationships, family, and emotional expression. All of these needs must be met, and if any of them are missing, you will be left with a weakened sense of self. A strong sense of self is what gives people the strength to go on in the world and make sense of things. People who are missing the lower parts of the triangle will find that they are more prone to being manipulated.

If we take this to the most literal level, imagine if you are starving. You live in a place where there is very little food, and it is work just to be able to eat every day. Imagine someone comes along and says that if you join their religion or club, you will be fed every day. Of course, you will join their club, because you need food. The other parts don't matter. You don't really have a good choice here; the best choice is to join up and do whatever is required of you to be a part of the club so that you are able to get food and water every day.

This is true for the rest of the pyramid as well. This happens to people who are lacking a family system. If you don't have a family system, you are not able to feel secure in the world. This makes people more susceptible to joining cults and other organizations that take advantage of people. Cults often prey on the weak and lonely, and they offer up a place to have family and a place where they can find support in their lives, rather than being alone. The cult uses this as a manipulation tactic to make the person think a certain way. After the cult has gained enough followers, they are able to have power. Each person adds to the leader's power. The reason that people are recruited is that they are missing one of the levels of the pyramid of needs. Each person needs a family and a system of support, and if they don't have that, they are more easily manipulated.

So, in the grand scheme of things, you should always be working towards self-realization. This will ensure that you have a life path that is working toward your own health and success.

Communication

Let's talk for a moment about communication. Communication is a huge part of being an effective leader, and it is very important if you want to have charisma and confidence. We use words to describe things, people, feelings, attitudes, theories, philosophies, and so on. We can choose many different words to describe the same thing- and this is where the trouble often starts. Let's say the foreman says that the shop assistant made an unfortunate decision. The union members in the shop assume he means that the assistant made the wrong decision. It is quite obvious to them that the foreman is being unfair by criticizing the assistant. The foreman counters by saying that it would be best if the men just forget the whole matter.

"Forget it" is something you say to someone when you get fed up with their inability to see and accept your point of view. It is often the same as saying "I can't get through to you. You're either too stupid or too stubborn to see the truth." Yet the foreman may simply have been expressing his desire to escape from an unexpected conflict. The whole problem here was the failure by both sides to correctly interpret the relationship between the words and the reality.

Man has advanced through the use of language, but for the same reason, the complexity of human language has created many of his problems. There would be less misunderstanding if each object and feeling had only one single word to describe it. This is not the case and is suspect that we are rather glad that that is not the case. However, recognition and acceptance of this verbal communication problem is the first step in overcoming it.

Each person, object, or idea can be described by many different words, and each word might well trigger a unique response from every person to whom it is directed. This process is easy to understand if we can accept the idea of the human mind being much like a computer. Information can be fed into a computer and stored there for future reference. The human mind works the same way. The mind is the storehouse of information and attitudes which are stockpiled there as the result of all past experiences.

Much of the information stored in the human mind may never be used; the conscious mind may not even be aware of the existence of some of the information kept in the dark recesses of the subconscious, but nevertheless, it is there. When you hear the word Siberia, what comes into your mind? Bitter cold? Desolation? Chances are good that you have never actually been to Siberia, but past experiences – what you have read, heard, and seen in pictures- have been stored in your mental computer. The word Siberia is fed into that computer and you respond with a mental image of the place called Siberia which is distinctly your own and may be quite unlike that of another person.

Our failure to recognize the arbitrary relationship between the word and the object (that the word is not the thing) is made clear at one point in the novel Bread and Wine by Ignazio Silone. There is a scene in the book involving some men playing a card game called the settemezzo. In this game, the kind of diamonds is the key card and their particular kind of diamonds is worn out from handling and is easily recognizable. One of the players suggests substituting the three of spades for the card. A heated discussion erupts because of the players' claims such a substitution would be impossible. He flatly says: "The king of diamonds is always the king of diamonds. He may be filthy, torn, or have holes in him, but he's still the king of diamonds.

We also make the mistake of thinking that words can give us certain guarantees. We assume that fine-sounding word guarantees quality. You think not? If you were to drive into a strange town while on a trip, and stopping for lunch, you noticed there were but two restaurants in town, which one would you choose: Mom's Place or Ptomaine Corners? Chances are, you would choose Mom's Place, simply because the name seems to give you a certain guarantee.

This brings us to the definitions of connotation and denotation. The sharpest denotation would be the thing itself, the object. Since we are speaking of language, we must apply denotation to the world of words and infer that denotation is the factual language we use to describe something. Denotation is best exemplified by the dictionary definition. It is the connotative language that we are most interested in because it is the language we most often use.

In order to become the type of person who is able to use their Machiavellian confidence, you must be a person who understands this material and is able to use it for your advantage. A person with Machiavellian confidence knows how to communicate. Think about how much communication has evolved in the past couple of decades. Rather than spending time writing out books and papers as previous generations did, younger people these days have less impetus than ever to engage their writing skills and actually create something that is of value. Gone, too, is the power of verbal communication. FI you visited universities in the 1970s and '80s and had conversations with the students, you would notice a marked difference from the communication skills that are presented in students today. It is just a fact that social media has greatly reduced people's capacity for strong verbal communication.

So, you, as a Machiavellian, should be able to master this realm of communication. When you say something, you should say it clearly and directly. Say what you mean the way you want to be perceived. You cannot be afraid to express yourself. This is what confidence is all about: expressing yourself. If you have fear about expressing yourself, you should look deeper into that fear and see where it is emanating from. Is it that you are afraid of being judged?

If it is the fear of being judged, you have to address this. Nobody's judgment can be put above your own. You must be your own god in the world. You must place your judgment above everyone else's in the entire world.

You Are What You Think

Ever heard the expression, "you are what you eat"? There is a variation on that phrase that I enjoy it goes: "You are what you think". When you think negative thoughts about yourself, you are participating in a sort of self-loathing self-fulfilling prophecy. If you are always telling yourself that you are lazy and worthless, you encourage yourself to do types of behaviors that you consider worthless or lazy. You start to think about yourself as the worst version of yourself. This is something that needs to be battled against. Positive thinking is much better for your overall health. Positive thinking will improve hour mood and attention span and even your physical health.

IT starts with a perspective change. You must think about yourself, what do I criticize about myself? Why do I criticize myself? You've gone to first identify the ways in which you bring yourself down. This may be an easier process for some than others. Some people have body issues. They don't like the way they look, or they find that they are continually putting themselves and possibly others down for their looks in its extreme, this is known as body dysmorphic disorder. This type of person will need to learn how to do two things: The first is to decide what they want to do, and are actually capable of doing, about their looks. This could be a practice of starting to jog or some other form of exercise. It could involve eating better. Whatever goes down, it just has to be something attainable and gentle. The second task is to let go of whatever you are holding that is negative about your appearance. You can just let that go and say, "I've been exercising lately, which is something that I can do to improve my appearance. That is enough work for me to do in this area." and forgive the rest. You've got to face that voice that is telling you to look horrible and disgusting because that voice is essentially just you. Sometimes we have bullies or abusive people in your lives, and they tell us to mean things about ourselves. Often, though it is coming from our own consciousness.

Positive thinking means that you are shifting from the perspective of bleakness and gloominess and starting to acknowledge the beautiful things that you do experience often times, it is o that there aren't beautiful experiences in our lives, but rather than we are not accessing the experiences that are right in front of us. Positive thinking means shifting just a little, fro "ugh, its dark out today and I don't want to go to work" to "its dark out today, but I am going to do my best at work and maybe take a nap afterward." It is not all sunshine and rainbows. The positive thing should be realistic and attainable.

Confidence will be greatly strengthened when you get into positive thinking. Confidence is something that is difficult to measure and difficult to grow. It comes from deep down in the spirit, and it knows that one can be kept safe and sound by his or her own will. Confidence comes from self-security. If there are a bunch of things that you hold in shame, like past experiences, or other sources of embarrassment, you will not find it easy to have confidence. To have confidence, you must let all that stuff go and admit to yourself that you are a person who is worthy of being listened to, hear, and understood, and then communicate yourself that way.

The best and most classic way to be confident is to be yourself and to own it. If you are a tall person, love that you are tall and share it with the world. If you are a short person, own it and love your shortness. There are all kinds of body traits and all kinds of people who love people with your body traits. Whatever mental or physical traits you might have insecurities about, you just have to give up on those anxieties and let go. This will better you in the long run. Motivation is extremely important to address for people with depression. Depression in large part very dependent on motivation. The lack of motivation is what drives depression, and often times this turns into a cycle of lack of motivation and negative feelings. Motivation is a nebulous concept, but we can pretty much say with confidence that when your body is healthier, you are generally more motivated. When you are spending all of your time on addiction or in unhealthy habits, you are feeding this cycle and your motivation will be cut short. This is unfortunate, but it happens.

A big part of positive thinking is learning to self-talk about good things and also to separate yourself from the bad thoughts. You can just let yourself know that thoughts are not real. You don't have to disprove thoughts, you can just say that they are mean or unnecessary and do away with them. Lots of people out there pace way to much value on their thoughts, their tiny little thoughts, and their content, and they spend all of their time "strategically" thinking, as to bring out some kind of satisfaction. But the satisfaction never comes.

What is helpful for this situation is to learn how to tell yourself declarations. You are not your thoughts. Your thoughts only exist in your head. Sometimes they are correct, or true, and sometimes they are not. It doesn't matter. In either case, they do not make you up. You are not a good person or a bad person for what you think.

Conclusion

Thank you for making it through to the end of *Dark Persuasion*, let's hope it was informative and able to provide you with all of the tools you need to achieve your goals whatever they may be.

The next step is to apply these concepts in your daily life and make observations. Just remember, this might be the first step. As you grow more aware of the psychological principles that are happening around you, you will be more powerful in your inner life and also in relationships.

CPSIA information can be obtained
at www.ICGtesting.com
Printed in the USA
LVHW020302041120
670574LV00003B/444

9 781801 139564